D1612118

RAND

An Overview and Comparison of Demand Assignment Multiple Access (DAMA) Concepts for Satellite Communications Networks

Phillip M. Feldman

Prepared for the
United States Air Force

Project AIR FORCE
1946 - 1996

Preface

This report provides a broad survey of demand assignment multiple access (DAMA) techniques for satellite communications. The primary intended audiences are military planners, communications system designers and architects, and the military acquisition community at large. However, much of the material in this report will also be of interest for commercial communications system planners and designers, especially where there is a potential for military use of these commercial systems.

The report describes a wide (but not exhaustive) set of DAMA techniques, with emphasis on those techniques that offer the greatest practical benefit for military applications. Methods for making DAMA systems resistant to interference and jamming are discussed, including some new methods.

The report covers both pure DAMA protocols, which efficiently handle voice traffic and long data transmissions, and hybrid DAMA protocols, which can efficiently handle not only voice and long data transmissions, but also short data transmissions (packets). Because of the increasing importance of packetized communications for the military, an entire chapter is devoted to the subject of hybrid DAMA.

Selected performance results are presented, including some new performance results. To make the material in this report accessible to readers with only a basic background in communications, a substantial amount of tutorial material has been included.

This research was performed for a project on "Space and C^{3}I Systems" in the Force Modernization and Employment Program of Project AIR FORCE and was sponsored by the Air Force Space Command (AF/SC).

Project AIR FORCE

Project AIR FORCE, a division of RAND, is the Air Force federally funded research and development center (FFRDC) for studies and analyses. It provides the Air Force with independent analyses of policy alternatives affecting the development, employment, combat readiness, and support of current and future aerospace forces. Research is being performed in three programs: Strategy and

Doctrine, Force Modernization and Employment, and Resource Management
and System Acquisition.

In 1996, Project AIR FORCE is celebrating 50 years of service to the United States
Air Force. Project AIR FORCE began in March 1946 as Project RAND at Douglas
Aircraft Company, under contract to the Army Air Forces. Two years later, the
project became the foundation of a new, private nonprofit institution to improve
public policy through research and analysis for the public welfare and security of
the United States—what is known today as RAND.

Contents

Figures

Tables

Summary

Demand Assignment Multiple Access (DAMA) is a class of multiple-access techniques that permit a population of users to share satellite resources on a demand basis. The need for flexible local and long-haul communications by mobile military users is increasing rapidly. Radio nets cannot provide the long-haul connectivity and, for the most part, do not support point-to-point communications. Thus, only satellite communications can meet the needs of these mobile users. DAMA permits more efficient and flexible allocation of limited satellite resources.

The DAMA control can be distributed, centralized, or hierarchical. Although DAMA with fully distributed control has been used with some commercial satellites (e.g., the SPADE system on INTELSAT IV), centralized and hierarchical control are better suited for military applications because of the need to handle prioritized traffic (multiple precedence levels). In systems with centralized control, the resource controller can be located either in a special ground terminal or in the satellite itself. Putting the resource controller in the satellite increases the complexity of the satellite but offers significant performance benefits, especially for satellites with multiple beams.

All DAMA systems must provide a return orderwire (ROW) via which users can request assignments from the resource controller. A variety of contention protocols have been proposed for management of the ROW ("ROW access"). Every contention protocol has a characteristic maximum throughput; when the request arrival rate exceeds this limit, the backlog of users waiting for assignments begins to grow linearly with time, and some users wait indefinitely to receive assignments. This maximum throughput varies from 18 percent for some of the simplest protocols, to almost 50 percent for the most sophisticated ones. Most systems currently in use, or planned, use a form of slotted Aloha, for which the maximum throughput is roughly 36 percent. Thus, there is the potential for significant increases in ROW efficiency.

Slotted Aloha suffers from a form of instability that can cause occasional long delays even when request arrival rates are less than the maximum throughput. Ways of modifying slotted Aloha to eliminate this instability have been found. However, there is another class of contention protocols, the splitting protocols, which are inherently stable, and which also provide higher maximum throughput than that of slotted Aloha.

A wide variety of DAMA resource allocation schemes have been proposed, including pure FDMA/DAMA, pure TDMA/DAMA, and hybrids of DAMA with other multiple access techniques such as contention and reservations. The pure DAMA protocols are best suited for traffic consisting only of voice and long data transmissions (e.g., file transfers and faxes). For systems that must transmit not only voice and long data files, but also short data messages (packets), pure DAMA is inefficient because the overhead associated with connection setup and termination becomes excessive for these short messages. As the military moves toward packet communications ("digitized forces"), the mix of traffic will increasingly shift toward packetized data. Hybrid DAMA protocols, although more complex than pure DAMA, are preferable for user traffic that contains a mix of voice and long data transmissions with short data transmissions. Further attention to and investigation of hybrid DAMA are needed because of the potential for increased packet data throughput for given satellite resources.

Without protection at the waveform level, DAMA systems are highly vulnerable to jamming and unintentional interference. A jammer with power comparable to that of a user terminal can disable an entire DAMA system by jamming the ROW, preventing users from sending requests to the resource controller. A number of approaches for making DAMA systems more jam resistant are discussed in this report, including some new methods. Techniques include the use of frequency hopping or direct sequence spread spectrum for the ROW, either in a separate band, or over the same band as the user channels. Another possibility is to permute all of the channels of an FDMA/DAMA system using frequency hopping spread spectrum. Use of simulation to quantify some of the performance trade-offs remains to be done. In particular, it has been conjectured that slotted Aloha is less vulnerable to jamming than the splitting protocols, but this has not been established.

Traditional analyses of circuit-switched networks assume that users who are blocked (refused a channel assignment because all channels are in use) never reattempt the call. In practice, this is not a reasonable assumption; users whose calls are critical are likely to try again and again until they get a connection. Our results show that accounting for these reattempts causes the predicted behavior of the system to change dramatically. When reattempts are ignored, the blocking probabilities increase gradually with the new request arrival rate. When reattempts are modeled, there is a maximum new request rate that can be tolerated; when this limit is reached, the protocol collapses, i.e., the blocking probability becomes 100 percent. We have found that high request rates (approaching or exceeding the call-handling capacity of the system), which must be expected under crisis conditions, can produce blocking probabilities that are much larger than would be predicted using a model that ignores reattempts.

When user request rates increase to the point that blocking probabilities and/or delays are excessive, some form of congestion control must be employed. One congestion control mechanism currently used in military DAMA implementations is priority queueing; higher precedence (higher priority) requests jump ahead of pending requests from lower precedence users, and calls of lower precedence users may also be terminated prematurely to free channels.

When the volume of high precedence traffic exceeds system capacity, or when it is unacceptable to deny access to all but the highest precedence users, priority queueing must be supplemented with other types of congestion control. For hybrid DAMA systems, several types of congestion control are possible that are not available for pure DAMA systems. One of the new methods that we propose is to restrict types of communications that require higher data rates. For example, when the system is overloaded, one might force all but the highest precedence users to use store-and-forward voice and text messages instead of interactive, two-way voice. Congestion control mechanisms that force users to economize are preferable to mechanisms that deny access.

Acknowledgments

Had it not been for the help of many people who gave generously of their time, this report would be far less accurate, complete, and intelligible. I would like to give special thanks to Edward Bedrosian and Gaylord Huth of RAND, to Joseph Han of AirTouch Communications, Inc., and to Professor Alan Konheim of the University of California at Santa Barbara for their extensive comments on the drafts. Comments from Roberto Garcia of the Aerospace Corp. were also helpful. Individuals whose work I discuss and who helped me to understand their papers include Jeffrey Wieselthier of the Naval Research Laboratory and Joseph Aein of RAND.

1. Introduction

1.1 Scope and Audience

Demand assignment multiple access (DAMA) is a loosely defined class of circuit- and packet-switched multiple-access techniques. Although DAMA techniques have found applications in satellite networks, local area networks (LANs), and other types of networks, this report addresses only the satellite applications. DAMA implementations include both military and commercial communications networks; the number of standards activities and developmental systems suggest that a rapid increase in DAMA implementations will occur over the next few years.

The need for flexible local and long-haul communications by mobile military users is increasing rapidly. Cellular phone systems require base stations and other fixed ground infrastructure. Radio nets cannot provide the long-haul connectivity and for the most part do not support point-to-point communications. Thus, only satellite communications can meet the needs of these mobile users. DAMA techniques permit a population of mobile users to efficiently share satellite resources on a demand basis.

In this report, we attempt to provide the broadest possible survey of DAMA techniques, together with a selected set of performance results. The primary foci of the report are description and explanation of the different DAMA approaches and discussion of performance and implementation issues, including some high-level design trade-offs. Existing systems and standards are mentioned only as examples of the techniques and are not discussed in detail. Most of the performance results that we present are taken from the published literature, but a few new results have been included to cover cases of general interest that were not previously explored.

We assume some familiarity with communications engineering concepts and terminology. We frequently draw on the results and analytical methods of queueing theory and of multiple-access communications, but we do not assume any background in these areas; instead, we present an extensive glossary of terms and in Appendix A we present a tutorial review of queueing terminology, notation, and concepts.

1.2 Multiple Access Communications

In a multiple access system, users transmit information (e.g., voice or data) to one another using a shared communications medium. This shared medium could take any of several forms. The following are three examples of multiple access systems. In a mobile satellite system with a single earth-coverage beam, ground terminals transmit to the satellite using one frequency band; the satellite rebroadcasts the signal using a different frequency band. All terminals (including the sender) hear the rebroadcast after a delay that includes the two-way propagation time and any processing delays. In a LAN, two or more computers are connected to a common bus (coaxial cable or fiber optic cable). If one computer transmits a message, all other computers hear the transmission after a delay. In a packet radio system for mobile users (manpack radios or radios on ground vehicles), a user's transmission can be received by other users within some range that depends on the transmit power level and other factors.[1]

Although the shared medium is quite different in the above examples, a common feature of all three systems is that when any single user transmits, many other users can receive the transmission. In a mobile satellite system, users receive all transmissions from other users. A full-duplex radio can also monitor the rebroadcast of its own transmission. A half-duplex radio can do this only if the sum of the transmission duration and the *turnaround time* (time for the radio to switch from send mode to receive mode) is less than the round-trip delay. In the LAN, users receive all transmissions except their own. In the packet radio system, in general, each user can receive the transmissions of some subset of the user population (this subset is different for each receiver, and "A can hear B" does not imply "B can hear A"). For any of these systems, suppose that user A can receive transmissions from B and C, and that B and C transmit messages during overlapping time intervals. Unless strong forward error correction coding is being used, an overlap of only a few bits is sufficient to practically guarantee the loss of both messages, i.e., nothing intelligible is received; this event is called a *collision*.[2]

A multiple access protocol is an algorithm that coordinates user transmissions, including transmission of new packets and resolution of collisions (for protocols that permit collisions). Over the last few decades, a wide variety of multiple access communications protocols have been proposed for different combinations

---

[1]Most military radios lack the capability for packet/burst transmission. However, newer radios will have this capability.

[2]In some systems, the more powerful of two signals will "capture" the receiver and be correctly received; we ignore this possibility here.

of operating environments, patterns of usage, and user requirements. Why are there so many different multiple-access schemes? Part of the explanation is that protocols that are suitable for some applications are often inadequate for other applications. Issues that must be considered in the selection or design of a multiple-access protocol include the following:

- What is the mean duration of a message transmission or of a call? In particular, the ratio of this duration to propagation delay is of fundamental importance.

- Do users generate messages or calls at fairly regular times, or in a "bursty" (irregular) fashion?

- What is the distribution of message length or of the call holding time? (Call holding times always have some variability; message lengths may be either fixed or variable.)

- How critical is delay? In some applications, e.g., file transfer, only the time at which the last piece of a file is received is of interest, and even this may not be very critical. For packetized voice, packets must be delivered with low, nearly constant delay. For some message traffic, there is no hard limit on delay, but the value of the message may fall off rapidly with increasing delay.

- Are user equipments (terminals) operating in a benign environment, or are high levels of noise, interference, or jamming present?

- To what extent can a message or call tolerate lost packets or corrupted bits?

- For systems that must support traffic of different types, e.g., voice, file transfers, and short data transmissions, the mix of these traffic types is generally important.

In the remainder of this report, we consider only multiple access schemes that are appropriate for satellite communications.

1.3 Basic Waveform Types

There are many possible ways to share a given band of frequencies among a population of users. The basic waveform types are:

- Time division multiple access (TDMA). Time is divided into slots, typically of fixed length, as shown in Figure 1. A given transmission must fall entirely within a single slot. Slots are grouped into frames. The kth slot in every frame is assigned to a given user.

4

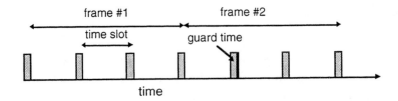

Figure 1—Time Division Multiple Access (TDMA)

- Frequency division multiple access (FDMA). The band is divided into smaller non-overlapping frequency sub-bands, or channels, as shown in Figure 2. A given transmission uses only one of these channels.

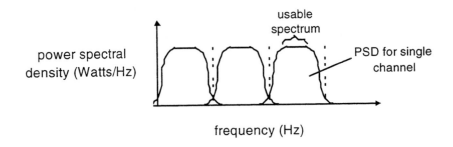

Figure 2—Frequency Division Multiple Access (FDMA)

- Frequency-hop spread spectrum. Both time and frequency are subdivided; each transmission uses a specific pseudo-random sequence of frequency slots (the "hopping pattern"), as shown in Figure 3. Gray squares in the figure correspond to a single hopping pattern.

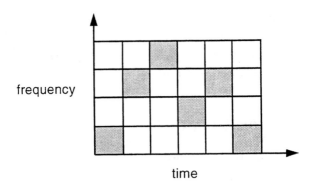

Figure 3—Frequency Hop Spread Spectrum

- Direct-sequence (DS) spread spectrum. A bit stream can be viewed as a binary function, i.e., a continuous-time function that takes on the values 0 and 1. Consider a user data stream having bit rate R_u. Prior to modulation, this stream is exclusive OR'd with a pseudo-random bit stream having rate $R_p \gg R_u$. The output stream is modulated and transmitted. This sequence of operations is shown in Figure 4. The resulting spread spectrum waveform has a bandwidth that is larger than that of the unspread waveform by a factor R_p / R_u.

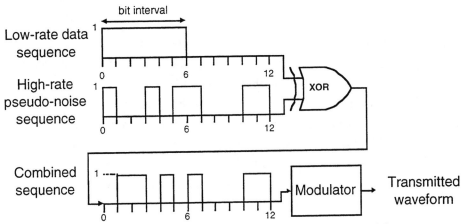

Figure 4—A Possible Implementation for Direct Sequence Spread Spectrum
(transmit side only)

With either FH or DS spread spectrum, a given transmission typically uses the entire band of frequencies over the duration of the transmission but can, nevertheless, cause minimal interference to other users in the same band (and incur minimal interference from them). Combinations of these waveform types are also possible. For further discussion, we refer the reader to Ziemer and Peterson (1985).

1.4 Contention, Reservations, and Other Multiple Access Schemes

Consider, for the moment, the TDMA waveform type of the previous subsection. If two users transmit in the same slot, both transmissions are garbled and nothing intelligible is received; this is called a *collision*. There are a variety of approaches for dealing with this possibility; four basic classes of methods are particularly important:

Fixed TDMA Assignments

Time is divided into frames, each of which contains a fixed number of slots, and each user has one or more assigned slots per frame. A given user may transmit only in his assigned slots. A given slot belongs to only one user. Thus, for a population of m users, there must be at least m slots in the frame. This method avoids collisions entirely but imposes high delays unless m is small. Fixed TDMA assignments are wasteful unless most users have something to transmit in their assigned slots.

TDMA with Contention

In these protocols, which include slotted Aloha and splitting protocols, there are no assigned slots. (If there is a frame structure, the number of slots per frame may be much smaller than the number of users.) Users contend for slots, and any collisions that ensue must be resolved in some manner. Delays in the delivery of packets from user A to user B will tend to vary randomly, with delays much longer than the mean delay occurring occasionally (due to variation in the offered traffic from other users and in the incidence of collisions). For packetized, real-time, interactive voice (the packet analog of full-duplex voice), user satisfaction depends on delivery of packets at a relatively fixed rate, and fixed assignment TDMA is thus more suitable than contention schemes for such applications. Note, however, that contention schemes may be preferable for delivery of store-and-forward (noninteractive) voice and text messages, or other data. See subsections 3.2–3.4 for further discussion of contention schemes.

TDMA Reservation Protocols

Like fixed assignment TDMA, reservation schemes prevent collisions. In the simplest TDMA reservation protocol (Bertsekas and Gallager, 1992), each frame consists of a *status slot* followed by a variable number of data slots. Each status slot, which is not necessarily the same length as other slots in the frame, consists of n *minislots*. Each minislot is associated with a particular user, so that n equals the number of users in the system. Figure 5 shows the frame structure for n = 6 (an unrealistically small value).

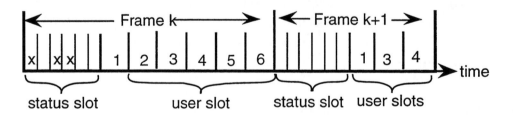

Figure 5—Reservation Frame Structure

A minislot allows for an extremely short transmission that conveys no data, but that must be distinguishable from background noise with high probability. By transmitting in his assigned minislot in frame k, a user signals the other users in the system that he requires a data slot in frame k+1. In Figure 5, an "x" in a minislot indicates a transmission. Since three users transmitted reservations in frame k, there are three user slots in frame k+1. Each user slot is labeled with the identification number of the user who transmitted during that slot.[3]

To guarantee that all users will have heard the rebroadcast of frame k's status slot by the time they finish transmitting frame k+1's status slot, the duration of a frame may not be less than the two-way propagation delay (this can be achieved by inserting "fill" slots at the end of any frame that would otherwise be too short). Reservation schemes may be attractive when a relatively small, fixed-size population of users requires high throughput and bounded delays.

TDMA with Contention for Reservation

This is similar to the previous approach, except that the minislots are not assigned to specific users, which allows the number of minislots to be smaller than the number of users. A user who wants a slot transmits an identifying sequence of bits in one of the minislots. If no other user transmitted in that minislot, the reservation is successful, and the next frame will contain a slot assigned to the user who placed the reservation. This approach is attractive when the size of the user population is so large that conventional TDMA reservation minislots would use too large a fraction of the frame. It permits higher throughput than can be attained with pure contention, at the expense of increased delay. See Lee and Mark (1983) for further discussion.

Combinations of these approaches are possible. It is common to build more complex protocols using simpler protocols as components. As we shall see, the simpler DAMA protocols are essentially combinations of FDMA, fixed TDMA assignments, and TDMA with contention.

---

[3]Our labeling of the user slots implies that user 1 will always transmit in the first user slot of a frame whenever he has something to transmit. More generally, user i will experience lower mean delay than user j, for i < j. This unfair situation can be remedied by permuting the order of the users, with a different permutation being used for each frame, and all permutations occurring with the same frequency.

8

1.5 FDMA/DAMA and TDMA/DAMA

Because of the lack of a universally accepted definition for DAMA, the term has been applied to multiaccess schemes that are substantially different. FDMA/DAMA, the classical and simplest form of DAMA, is illustrated in Figure 6.

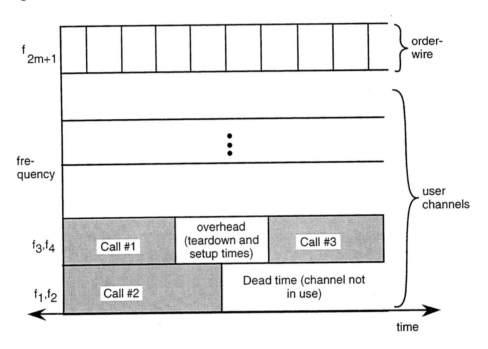

Figure 6—FDMA/DAMA

The available satellite frequency bandwidth is divided (FDMA) into 2m+1 channels, with guard bands between adjacent channels so that interference due to power spillover remains within acceptable levels (guard bands are not shown in the figure). The pool of available channels is shared by a large population of users (>>m) who have unpredictable needs for the resource, i.e., the users cannot specify beforehand precisely when they will need access and to whom, thus precluding fixed assignment FDMA (a scheme in which channels are permanently assigned to specific connections or users, analogous to fixed assignment TDMA).

One channel, which is called the *orderwire*, permits the exchange of control information such as call requests and channel assignments between a *resource controller* and the users it serves. The orderwire is typically divided using a combination of fixed TDMA assignments and TDMA with contention; some slots are reserved for the controller, while user requests contend for the remaining slots. Users communicate in pairs, transmitting two-way (full-duplex) voice on an assigned pair of channels for some period of time, and then terminating the connection and releasing the channels for use by others.[4] With 2m+1 channels, the system can support m full-duplex connections.

In TDMA/DAMA, also called packet DAMA, a single channel is divided into nonoverlapping time intervals called *frames*. Each frame is further subdivided into some number of fixed-length *slots*. Figure 7 shows a simple form of TDMA/DAMA in which each frame consists of m slots: one forward orderwire (FOW) slot, k≥1 return orderwire (ROW) slots, and m – k – 1 user slots (k varies from frame to frame, but m remains fixed). Figure 7 shows a possible TDMA/DAMA frame structure for the case m=8. "F" denotes an FOW slot, "R" a ROW slot, and "U" a user slot.

Figure 7—Possible Frame Structure for TDMA/DAMA

Users request a connection (assignment of a slot) or terminate a connection by transmitting a message to a resource controller; this request message is transmitted in one of the ROW slots on a contention basis. The resource controller announces assignments and provides other status information using the FOW slot. In the example of Figure 7, the termination of a connection in frame l frees a user slot, which is converted into a ROW slot in frame l+1. Each of the user slots in a frame is associated with a particular connection, i.e., from user A to user B. For some connections, more than one slot per frame may be assigned. Thus, we see that TDMA/DAMA has the flexibility to support connections with widely different transmission rates.

TDMA/DAMA is similar to TDMA with contention for reservations, which we discussed in the previous subsection. There is, however, an important difference: TDMA/DAMA allocates one or more slots per frame to an ongoing connection, whereas TDMA with contention for reservations allocates a single slot in a single frame, i.e., a user must make a new reservation each time he requires another slot.

---

[4]In a static assignment scheme that associates one channel with each possible destination (or source), the number of channels must equal the number of users. If, as is commonly the case, most users have nothing to say most of the time, static assignment is very wasteful of bandwidth and scarce hardware resources.

1.6 DAMA Resource Allocation Schemes and Control Locales

A wide variety of DAMA resource allocation schemes have been proposed in the literature. DAMA protocols based on circuit switching alone, which we will refer to as *pure DAMA*, were designed to support two-way voice connections. Newer *hybrid DAMA* protocols, which combine DAMA with other multiaccess techniques such as TDMA reservations or contention schemes like slotted ALOHA, have been designed to efficiently support a mix of voice, long data transmissions, and short data transmissions (packets).

Most DAMA schemes fall into one of the following general categories:

1. Pure FDMA/DAMA. Circuit-switched assignment of fixed-bandwidth channels.[5] The return orderwire is accessed using slotted TDMA contention.

2. Pure TDMA/DAMA. A single frequency band is divided into time frames, and frames are subdivided into slots. Some slots are used for the orderwire, and others are assigned to ongoing connections.

3. Hybrid FDMA/DAMA with TDMA contention. Some channels are available for circuit-switched assignment to ongoing connections (typically voice). Other channels are shared on a contention basis; these channels are typically used for text messages, data, and other connectionless traffic.

   3.1 The number of channels available for circuit-switched and contention access and for the orderwire are fixed.

   3.2 The total number of channels is fixed, but the resource controller may change the number available for circuit-switched access, for contention access, and for the orderwire according to demand. The three sets of channels are separated by two "movable partitions."

4. Hybrid TDMA/DAMA with slotted contention and/or reservations.

   4.1 In each frame, certain slots are available for circuit-switched assignment, whereas others are designated for user contention access and for reservations.

---

[5]In theory, assignment of variable bandwidth channels is also possible, and could support connections of two or more types, e.g., voice and video, requiring substantially different data rates. For example, in an FDMA/DAMA system with a large number of 5 kHz channels separated by 3 kHz guard bands, a voice connection could be assigned a single 5 kHz channel, while a reduced-frame-rate, compressed-video connection could use a 21 kHz channel consisting of three 5 kHz channels and the intervening guard bands. As far as we know, no variable rate FDMA/DAMA systems have been designed, probably because TDMA/DAMA supports multiple data rates with less complexity (see the discussion in subsection 2.2).

4.2   A modification of 4.1 permits data users to transmit on a contention basis in slots nominally designated for circuit-switched assignment whenever these slots are free.

Each of these categories permits considerable variation, and there are other possibilities that do not match any of these categories.

In addition to specifying how the resources can be assigned to different types of traffic, it is also useful to consider where and how the assignments are made (the "control locale"); the set of possibilities is

- distributed control
- centralized control
  - resource control from special ground terminal (network control terminal [NCT])
    a. automated (computer) control
    b. automated control with override capability
    c. human in control
  - automated control from satellite
    a. with reprogramming capability, i.e., new control software can be uploaded from a properly authorized ground terminal after authentication
    b. with override capability
- hierarchical control.

These choices of allocation scheme and control locale will be explained and their implications discussed in Section 2. Clearly, there are many possible combinations of allocation scheme and control locale; however, not all of these combinations make sense; for example, allocation scheme 3.2, in which the number of channels allocated between voice and data adapts according to demand, requires a centralized controller that can decide how many channels to allocate for each type of traffic and can notify the user population.

Of course, there are many important aspects of system design left unspecified by the control locale and resource allocation categories that we have defined, e.g., frequencies of operation and frequency plan, data rates, modulation and coding, power control, and characteristics of the request channel.

2. High-Level Implementation Issues and Design Trade-offs

2.1 Introduction

The DAMA system designer is presented with several types of trade-offs. Besides the usual cost/complexity vs. performance trade-offs, there are trade-offs involving complexity in the satellite versus complexity in the ground terminals. The investment in ground terminals tends to be large compared with that in the space segment because the number of terminal equipment pieces deployed is large, e.g., 300 for the Defense Satellite Communications System (DSCS) to 30,000 or more for the ultra-high frequency (UHF) manpacks, while the number of satellites is typically small, e.g., 4 to 20. However, design choices are often motivated by the desire to minimize the initial investment rather than the total system life-cycle cost. Budget constraints usually force system designers to choose backward compatibility for interoperability over future performance and allowance for future flexibility and growth. For example, satellites with DAMA-specific onboard processing and buffering (see subsection 2.5) offer significant advantages over existing, primarily bent-pipe satellites. However, DAMA protocols that would make use of such onboard processing and buffering are not compatible with the current generation of satellites.

In the remainder of this section, we focus on selected high-level implementation and design alternatives, including qualitative discussion of performance and complexity trade-offs. Although complexity has cost implications, we do not explicitly discuss cost. In subsection 2.2, we compare FDMA/DAMA and TDMA/DAMA. In subsection 2.3, we take an initial look at pure DAMA versus hybrid DAMA; a more detailed assessment of hybrid DAMA and its advantages over pure DAMA is given in Section 5. In subsection 2.4, we define three alternative resource control locales and explain their implications. Satellites with multiple-beam antennas and onboard processing and buffering are discussed in subsections 2.5 and 2.6, respectively. Subsection 2.7 offers some solutions to the problem of congestion control. Subsection 2.8 explains some of the factors involved in the selection of a slot size for a TDMA/DAMA system.

2.2 FDMA/DAMA Versus TDMA/DAMA

TDMA permits more flexible allocation of capacity than FDMA. For example, in a TDMA system, one might assign one slot per frame to a low-rate connection (e.g., for voice), and several slots per frame to a higher-rate connection (e.g., for video). When available bandwidth is subdivided into channels via FDMA, one may not be able to freely change the widths and locations of the channels because some satellites have fixed channelizing filters. Even for satellites that do not have channelizing filters, dynamic adaptation of the frequency plan is problematic because frequencies and power levels must be chosen to minimize intermodulation products (this is not an issue for TDMA). Also, FDMA generally requires Doppler correction.

TDMA, while providing more flexibility than conventional FDMA, is more complex to implement (users must be synchronized with the slot boundaries). More important, because users in a TDMA system transmit at low duty cycles, considerably higher transmitter peak Equivalent Isotropic Radiated Power (EIRP) and receiver antenna gain (G/T) are required than for FDMA transmission for the same average data rate. Higher peak EIRP requires a higher-power transmitter, larger antenna, or both, which in turn implies increased cost and weight.

For systems that must accommodate connections requiring widely differing data rates, a combination of FDMA and TDMA is more practical than FDMA or TDMA alone. One possible method for combining FDMA and TDMA (see Fang, 1982) is illustrated in Figure 8. The basic idea is to divide an entire transponder into frames using TDMA. Each frame is then further subdivided into two subframes. One subframe is shared by low-rate users on a FDMA basis; the second subframe is shared by high-rate users on a TDMA basis.

Suppose that there are 30 times as many low-rate users as high-rate users, but that each high-rate user requires 30 times the data rate of a low-rate user. In this case, the durations of the two subframes would be approximately equal. In this example, users are forced to burst at twice the rate that would be required if the entire band were divided into two subbands (instead of dividing each frame into two subframes). However, this small penalty may be offset by a savings in complexity, because changes in the traffic mix can be accommodated by simply shifting the boundary between the two subframes.

2.3 Pure DAMA Versus Hybrid DAMA

Before proceeding, we need to introduce some new terms:

- *Call setup time* is the time to establish a connection, including propagation delays and switching and other processing delays.

- *Call teardown time* is the time to close a connection, i.e., after the end of a call, the resource controller does not immediately become aware that the channel is free.

- *Call holding time* is the duration of the call from the moment that the connection is established until the termination of the call.

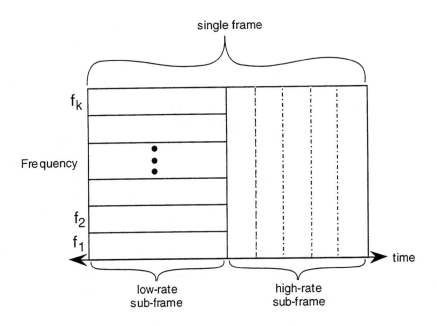

Figure 8—A Method for Combining TDMA and FDMA

For satellite systems that handle only voice traffic and that have call setup and teardown times on the order of 1 or a few seconds, pure DAMA, i.e., an allocation scheme based on circuit switching alone, can be quite efficient. The reason for this is that the call setup and teardown overhead tends to be short compared with the call holding times. Consider, for example, INTELSAT IV, which is at geostationary altitude. The mean connection setup time is approximately 2 seconds (Boag, 1969). Assuming a mean call holding time of 2 minutes, one finds that the call setup overhead is 2/(2+120)= 1.6 percent, i.e., call setup time overhead is acceptably small.[1]

However, for communications systems that must handle both voice and short data transmissions (e.g., text messages), pure DAMA may be inefficient. Assume that the channel information rate is 2.4 KB/sec, and that a typical message length is 800 bytes (ten 80-character lines of text). Under these assumptions, the "call holding time" is now only 2.67 seconds, in which case the overhead associated with the call setup time of 2 seconds is 2/(2+2.67)= 43 percent, an unacceptably high overhead. For a channel information rate of 4.8 KB/sec, the call setup overhead increases to 60 percent.

Hybrid DAMA protocols combine circuit-switched assignment with contention, reservations, scheduled transmission, or other techniques. For systems that must handle a mixture of traffic types, e.g., voice, long data transmissions, and short data transmissions, hybrid DAMA protocols increase throughput and reduce delay using such techniques as the following:

- Contention and reservation techniques eliminate call setup and teardown overheads and setup delay for data transmissions.

- Longer data transmissions can be scheduled, since the length of a message or file transfer is known in advance. This eliminates setup and teardown overheads (but not the setup delay).

- In a hybrid FDMA/DAMA system, channels not currently assigned to ongoing connections can be used for data transmissions on a contention basis.

- If voice is packetized, one may be able to send data packets during breaks in speech; see Weinstein (1983) and Rabiner (1994) for an overview of packetized voice and voice processing, respectively. It is estimated that a speaker is actually talking only 40 percent of the time in a typical two-way conversation (this is the "voice activation factor") (Evans, 1991). Inserting packets between breaks in speech is extremely efficient; however, because of the earth-to-satellite propagation delay (and the delay until the next break in speech), this approach requires buffering of packets on board the satellite (see subsection 2.5).

Hybrid DAMA protocols are discussed in detail in Section 5.

---

[1]For some military systems, the call setup times may be much longer than a few seconds. If call setup times are comparable to call holding times, efficiency would be quite low.

2.4 Control Locale

The selection of control locale is a high-level design decision that has important implications for other aspects of system design and for a variety of performance measures.

Centralized Control

In a centralized control scheme, all control functions reside in a single resource controller. Many military communications networks have been designed with centralized control. In designing a DAMA system with centralized control, one must decide where that control should reside, and whether channel assignments should be made manually by a human operator or automatically by a computer. The military has developed interoperability standards (standards applicable to all services) for 5-kHz and 25-kHz UHF DAMA systems (*Interoperability Standard for 5-kHz*, 1992; *Interoperability Standard for 25-kHz*, 1992); these standards specify centralized automatic control.

In many DAMA concepts, the resource controller is in a special ground terminal called a network control terminal (NCT). So that failure of this terminal does not render the system useless, there must be one or more NCT backups that can take over the functions of the primary NCT in the event of its destruction or failure (the backups continuously monitor the performance of the primary NCT).

For a simple DAMA architecture with a single satellite footprint covering all users and with the resource controller in an NCT, Figure 9 illustrates the sequence of transmissions involved in setting up and starting a call from user A to user B. Hops 1–2 transmit the request from user A to the NCT. If a channel is available, the NCT sends a channel assignment back to user A (hops 3–4). User A then begins transmitting to user B (hops 5–6). Note that this architecture imposes a minimum of three earth-satellite-earth round trip propagation delays (more if there are collisions) until user B receives the first bit of user A's transmission; processing and queueing in the NCT add to the delay.

Distributed Control

In a fully distributed DAMA system, all terminals make their own channel assignments. Distributed control is attractive from the standpoint of system reliability, because the failure of any number of terminals does not prevent the remaining terminals from continuing to communicate among themselves, i.e., there is no single point of failure except for the satellite itself.

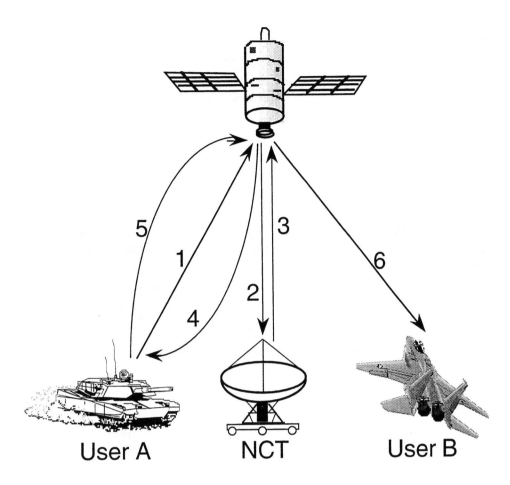

Figure 9—Sequence of Transmissions Required to Set Up and Initiate a Call from Terminal A to Terminal B for a System with the Resource Controller in an NCT

SPADE (Edelson and Werth, 1972), the earliest DAMA system implementation, was designed for use with INTELSAT IV satellites. INTELSAT satellites originally provided only trunking for international telephone calls; TV relay, regional trunking, and data relay were added later. SPADE was fully distributed, with every ground terminal having the capability to make channel assignments (this was a political necessity, because every national entity considered itself equal to all of the others).

There are some significant disadvantages to distributed control for circuit switched satellite communications. First, in most military communications systems and in some commercial ones, it is necessary to provide different grades of service for different users. For example, there may be high-precedence (high-priority) users who require preemptive access, i.e., it may be necessary to terminate a low-precedence call without waiting for its normal completion. This operation requires continual monitoring of all channel assignments, and a determination of which low-priority call is to be preempted when this is necessary. Although it is in theory possible to perform such operations in a distributed fashion, centralized control greatly simplifies the implementation of precedence- (and priority-)based resource allocation.

Second, all terminals must continuously monitor the request channel and keep track of which channels are in use at any time. In a scheme with centralized control, only the resource controller needs to keep track of what resources are in use. Third, if two users attempt to set up a circuit at the same time (or nearly the same time), conflicting assignments may result. This means that two terminals reserve the same channel and transmit simultaneously, such that interference between the two transmissions prevents either from being received. The possibility of conflicting assignments requires that the communications network protocol include a mechanism to detect and correct for such conditions; this involves some additional complexity (the SPADE system (Edelson and Werth, 1972) contains such a mechanism). In a properly operating system with centralized control, conflicting assignments are not possible.

Hierarchical Control

Hierarchical control represents an intermediate option between fully centralized control and fully distributed control. In this control scheme, control is divided among multiple ground controllers (NCTs), each of which manages a pool of channels assigned by a single master controller. As with fully distributed control, hierarchical control avoids a single systemwide point of failure. In addition, hierarchical control offers some important advantages over fully distributed control.

First, since each resource controller manages only a subset of the channels and users (and thus handles a lower volume of call requests), the memory and processing requirements at each resource controller are reduced.[2]

Second, for some communications systems, a pair of terminals that have an unobstructed line-of-sight (LOS) or that are sufficiently close can communicate directly without using the satellite, e.g., via LOS microwave or groundwave. At low antenna elevation angles, terrain obscuration limits interference to the immediate vicinity of the transmitter. Under these conditions, tactical UHF

---

[2]The total required memory and processing must increase, however, because one loses the benefit of the "statistical multiplexer effect," which results from pooling of user populations and servers, i.e., as the load on individual processors decreases, the relative variability in the individual load tends to increase.

radios can use the entire military UHF band (225 to 400 MHz), rather than being limited to the few MHz of bandwidth available in the UHF communications satellites, e.g., LEASAT, FLTSATCOM, or UFO (UHF follow on). In such situations, a local controller or commander in the vicinity could assign to a local net a channel that would not conflict with any of the satellite channels, thereby reducing the load on the satellite channels.

Third, only nodes responsible for resource control functions need to receive continuously to monitor the system status (keep track of what channels are in use) and respond to requests. Ordinary user equipment may be able to save a little power by being powered off. Turning the receiver off is an advantage for manpack equipment with limited battery life.[3]

As previously mentioned, many military communications networks have been designed with centralized control. There is, however, a super high frequency (SHF) DAMA standard developed by the Defense Information Systems Agency (DISA, 1993) that specifies an interesting form of hierarchical control. Each NCT manages a pool of resources for up to 512 terminals; each of these terminals can in turn act as an NCT for up to 512 other terminals that are subordinate to it. There is no limit to the degree of nesting.

With hierarchical control, there is some additional complexity associated with establishing connections between users controlled by different NCTs. If users can move between regions controlled by different NCTs, the NCTs must periodically exchange information about the locations of users; there is some network overhead associated with the dissemination of this information.

Manual Versus Automatic Channel Assignments

Regardless of whether control is centralized or hierarchical, channel assignments can be made either manually by human operators or automatically by computers. It is inadvisable for channel assignments to be routinely made by a human operator because human operators

- have slow and unpredictable response times
- tend to make mistakes under stress, precisely when fast and accurate assignments are most essential.

---

[3]In frequency hopping systems, the power consumption of the frequency synthesizer may be significant. Turning off the equipment saves power at the cost of delay on power up because of time synchronization and frequency tracking.

Automated channel assignment by a computer in the NCT, with a capability for operator override, would permit a human operator to handle any unusual situations that could not have been foreseen.

2.5 Multiple-Beam Satellites

Satellites with multiple-beam antennas or with multiple spot beams are attractive because they permit frequency reuse, i.e., the same frequencies can be used in nonadjacent beams, thereby permitting an increase in the level of traffic that can be supported. For military applications, the multiple-beam satellite also confers some resistance to jamming, since a jammer must either be inside the footprint of the beam to be jammed or have a substantial advantage in EIRP over user terminals.

For satellites with multiple-beam antennas, DAMA resource control can be managed in any of several ways, for example:

1. Each footprint contains its own NCT, and users communicate only with other users covered by the same footprint. This architecture is quite decentralized, but each NCT functions as an independent centralized DAMA resource controller within its own beam.

2. The satellite multiplexes or otherwise combines ROWs from all beams, downlinking them to a single master NCT. This is an example of fully centralized resource control.

3. The footprint of each beam contains an NCT. Communications between users in different beams are coordinated by a master NCT that communicates with all of the lower-level NCTs. This architecture, which is an example of hierarchical resource control, has the advantage that each individual NCT handles a lower volume of requests than the master NCT of 2 above. However, setup times will be greater for calls between users in different beams as a result of the extra two-way propagation delay.

4. The DAMA resource controller is on board the satellite. Benefits of this approach are explained in the next subsection.

Note that with option 1, user connectivity is severely limited. In options 2 and 3, the master NCT must be able to command the satellite to route specified channels between beams; control of the satellite switching would be problematic without a single master NCT. For a military system, the master NCT should be in a safe area, i.e., outside the theater of operations.

In commercial multiple-beam satellite systems for mobile satellite services (proposed or under development), all channel requests arriving at a given satellite are downlinked to one of the available earth stations. Earth stations are linked through a fiber optic network so that authentication and billing information can be exchanged. Connections between mobile users covered by different satellites or between mobile and nonmobile users are completed through the public switched telephone network.

2.6 Onboard Processing and Buffering

"Onboard processing" is usually associated with such techniques as the despreading of spread-spectrum signals, demodulation and remodulation, error correction decoding and reencoding, and adaptive beamforming. The benefits of these types of onboard processing are the same for both DAMA and non-DAMA systems.

DAMA-specific applications of onboard processing include putting a DAMA resource controller onboard the satellite, and, for multiple-beam satellites, packet switching between beams. Clearly, these types of capabilities increase the required processing and data storage capacities of the satellite. Over the past decade, however, there have been dramatic improvements in throughputs of general-purpose processors and capacity of solid-state memories, as well as in power consumption, reliability, and costs of both. Radiation-hard microprocessors with throughputs in the 1 to 4 MIPS range and memory boards with radiation-hard static RAM (random access memory) (SRAM) of 1 to 10 Mbits are readily available.[4,5] Use of solid-state processors and memories in communications satellites is expected to grow rapidly (Nelson, 1994; "Fast SRAMs," 1995; "Solid-State Gains Ground," 1995; McAuliffe, 1996). Estimated weights and power requirements associated with the processor, memory, and other components of an onboard packet switch can be found in (Zuk, 1995). (These parameters are for a specific onboard packet switch design and may not be applicable to other systems.) We now address some of the more important benefits of onboard processing and buffering for DAMA applications.

---

[4]The level of radiation that we refer to here is that encountered in normal operation of a spacecraft over the typical lifetime of 10 years or more.

[5]One-Mbit SRAMs are now available, and 4-Mbit SRAMs are expected to be available later this year (see Sewell, 1995). However, rad-hard 1-Mbit SRAMs suitable for use in a wide range of space applications are not yet available. According to McAuliffe (1996), Loral and Honeywell are in the final year of developing high-performance, rad-hard 1-Mbit SRAMs. Using multichip modules and the 1-Mbit SRAMs, one could construct space-qualified memory boards with capacities of 40 Mbits or more.

22

Onboard Resource Control

Onboard resource control has several merits. Call setup and initiation times are shorter, because one incurs only two earth-satellite-earth propagation delays instead of three (hops 2–3 in Figure 9 are eliminated). Call teardown delay is also reduced. As discussed before, the need for backup NCTs is eliminated (unless the onboard controller fails). The satellite is less likely to be destroyed than an NCT and, in any case, already represents a single point of system failure regardless of where the resource controller resides (unless more than one satellite is available). Also, there is a reduction in orderwire traffic. Channel requests need not be downlinked to the ground, and channel assignments and other status information are not uplinked to the satellite since they originate there. In addition, for satellites with multiple beams, setup of calls between users in different beams is simplified.

Having an onboard resource controller does not necessitate any loss of human control. High-level functions such as beam pointing or congestion management procedures can be handled by a ground controller, and a ground control would in any case always be able to upload new control software to the satellite should this be necessary, or as better protocols become available.

Onboard Packet Switching

For use of hybrid DAMA with a satellite having a multiple-beam antenna, or having several gimbaled spot-beam antennas, some type of packet switching is needed to forward packets on to the appropriate destinations (unless users are permitted to communicate only with other users in the same beam). This involves selecting the appropriate downlink beam, i.e., the beam whose footprint covers the intended recipient. Although packet switching can be done on the ground, putting both the packet switch and the DAMA resource controller onboard the satellite and integrating them together offer significant benefits. For example, insertion of packets into empty channels can be done more efficiently if downlink channel status information is available to the resource controller without propagation delay. Insertion of packets into speech gaps (see subsection 2.3) also becomes possible.

Onboard Buffering

In a pure DAMA system, there is no need to buffer user transmissions since a fixed transmission rate is allocated to the connection until it is torn down. However, buffering of requests at the resource controller is beneficial because waiting time variability is reduced, and the load on the request channel may also be reduced. This subject is explored further in Section 4.

On a multiple-beam satellite that handles packetized data with an onboard packet switch, arrivals of packets destined for users in the footprint of a particular beam will occasionally exceed the available downlink capacity on that beam. Thus, the satellite must be capable of buffering packets, i.e., storing them in memory until they can be transmitted. If the buffer is too small, many packets will be lost because of buffer overflow. In a well-designed system, the probability of packet loss due to buffer overflow should be comparable to or less than the probability of packet loss due to other causes, e.g., noise and interference.

For low-altitude satellites not connected by intersatellite links (crosslinks), buffering onboard the satellite permits the delivery of message traffic between users whose geographical separation prevents them from both being in view of the same satellite at the same time.

For satellites operating at frequencies around 8 GHz and above,[6] onboard buffering of messages and automatic repeat request (ARQ) can be used to minimize the effects of rain outages (Rafuse, 1980). This is particularly advantageous at higher frequencies, e.g., 44/20 GHz, and at lower elevation angles, e.g., less than 30 degrees elevation at the ground terminal, both of which significantly increase the excess path loss due to rain.

2.7 Congestion Management: Is Priority Queueing the Answer?

Military and commercial communications networks are generally designed to handle the predicted average traffic or the average daily peak traffic. However, crisis conditions tend to produce traffic levels (particularly within the crisis area) far greater than the average, which in turn produce network congestion. When call attempt rates exceed the system capacity (the average number of calls that can be handled per unit time), system performance can degrade to unacceptable levels. This means either blocking probabilities close to 100 percent, or, in systems with queueing of requests, long waiting times to get a circuit.

In military communications networks, the traditional hedge against the possibility of congestion has been to divide the users into precedence (priority)

---

[6]Rain loss is generally not a significant problem at frequencies below 4 GHz, even at elevation angles at the terminal as low as 5 to 10 degrees.

24

levels so that the highest precedence traffic is guaranteed tolerable response times. (See subsection A.8 for an overview of priority queueing). The DISA standard for SHF DAMA specifies a form of preemptive abort priority queueing in which a voice user who is about to be preempted (to free a circuit for use by a higher-precedence user) must be notified at least 30 seconds before the connection is terminated. As previously discussed, assignment of circuits according to head-of-line (HOL) priorities in practice requires a DAMA system with a centralized resource controller.

As one might expect, priority queueing reduces delays for high-priority users at the expense of increased delays for low-priority users. However, priority queueing can also result in a situation in which one or more of the lower classes of users receive no service at all. Results from queueing theory (see subsection A.8) show that this type of behavior is essentially unavoidable in priority-queueing systems unless some form of congestion management is used. Measured data confirm the theory. A report by N. E. Feldman and S. J. Dudzinsky, Jr. (1977) provides summary statistics for military traffic handled by the TACSAT satellite on a typical day of a crisis that continued for several months. Median waiting times were about 20 minutes for flash (high-precedence) messages, but on the order of several hours for some lower-precedence but urgent messages.

Fairly simple formulas permit one to predict the steady-state mean delay for each class of users in a single-server queueing system using HOL priorities, and to determine conditions under which a given class of users will experience long delays. Note that each available channel in an FDMA/DAMA system or slot in a TDMA/DAMA system can be assigned to a different circuit and thus must be considered a separate server. Unfortunately, no convenient analytical method exists for predicting delays in a multiple-server priority queueing system, i.e., one must use simulation. However, the conditions under which a class of users will experience long delays are essentially the same as for the single-server case: *When the total arrival rate of requests of classes k and above exceeds the system capacity, users with priorities less than or equal to k will not be served.*

Data from N. E. Feldman et al. (1979) indicate that under crisis conditions, as much as 60 percent of the traffic in certain military systems may be of precedence levels "operations immediate" or higher. When such a high percentage of the traffic is urgent, priority queueing is not by itself adequate as a mechanism for managing congestion.

Even when the volume of high-priority traffic is small, priority queueing at the resource controller does not guarantee that high-priority users will have small delays; they may not receive service at all. How can this happen? If the average request generation rate (of all priorities) exceeds the maximum throughput of the ROW, the ROW will collapse, so that most requests never reach the resource controller at all. An example of this is given in sub-subsection 4.7.4.

A variety of "congestion management" measures can be useful in circuit switched systems; we use this term to avoid confusion with "congestion control" and "flow control," which are used with packet switched systems (Bertsekas and Gallager, 1992).

In FDMA/DAMA systems, one can adapt the number of request channels according to the traffic arrival rate. At very high arrival rates, one may wish to reduce the number of request channels, since this makes more channels available for user communications and throttles down the number of requests flooding into the system (if the request arrival rate exceeds the maximum service rate, then there will in any case be unsatisfied requests). In commercial systems, where only the communications channels produce revenue, this type of congestion control is particularly attractive. See subsection 5.2 for discussion of a hybrid DAMA protocol that adapts the numbers of channels used for different functions.

In TDMA/DAMA systems that carry digital voice, the resource controller could command all vocoders to drop down to a lower rate, e.g., from 16,000 bps to 9,600, 4,800, or 2,400 bps. This would improve system availability at the expense of some loss of voice quality. To make use of this type of source rate control in an FDMA/DAMA system, one would need to be able to change channel widths and locations, which might not be practical (see the discussion at the beginning of subsection 2.2).

If the request arrival rate begins to approach the maximum throughput of the ROW, one must either adaptively increase the number of ROW channels, or choke off requests from lower-priority users. A special command could be transmitted on the FOW to shut off all lower-priority requests until further notice.

In systems that carry both voice and data, one could under extremely high demand exclude all voice traffic from the system, permitting only the use of messages, since one can handle a far greater volume of text messages than voice calls. See Section 5.3 for discussion of a hybrid DAMA protocol that permits this type of control.

It is sensible to design some spare capacity into communications networks to prevent the incidence of congestion in the first place. There are a variety of ways in which this can be done without using more spectrum or power; we mention only two of a large number of possible approaches:

- Use satellites with large numbers of spot beams to maximize the amount of frequency reuse (nonoverlapping beams may use the same frequencies without interference).

- Use spectrally compact modulations, e.g., minimum shift keying (MSK), sinusoidal frequency shift keying (SFSK), and trellis coded quadrature amplitude modulation (QAM). For example, the 99 percent power bandwidths of MSK and unfiltered quadrature phase shift keying (QPSK) are given by $1.2/T_b$ and $8/T_b$, respectively, where T_b is the channel bit time (Ziemer and Peterson, 1985). Thus, at equal channel rates, the 99 percent power bandwidth for MSK is 85 percent less than that of QPSK. In FDMA/DAMA systems, spectrally efficient modulation permits a substantial savings in guard band, i.e., channels can be packed closer together in frequency.

These methods are starting to find application in commercial and other nonmilitary systems and might also find application in some military systems in the near future.[7]

2.8 Slot/Packet Size Selection in TDMA/DAMA Systems

The choice of packet size has important consequences for performance of both pure and hybrid TDMA/DAMA protocols. Clearly, the selection of packet and slot sizes is essentially the same problem, since the length of a single packet is constrained by the slot duration.[8] As mentioned before, a slot must be large enough to accommodate a packet plus a small guard time.

Packet length affects voice quality in two ways:

- A voice packet cannot be transmitted until the last bit has left the vocoder, and cannot be played back until the last bit of the packet has been received. Total delay cannot exceed about 500 msec without impairing the interactivity of the connection. Since propagation delay for a geostationary satellite already accounts for about 250 msec, this means that a packet can contain at

---

[7]NASA's Advanced Communications Technology Satellite uses MSK modulation (Xiong, 1994).
[8]In theory, a packet can span multiple contiguous slots, but this is not done in practice.

most about 250 msec worth of speech, assuming that the transmission rate is much higher than the vocoder rate.

- Lost packets begin to impair intelligibility significantly when a single packet represents more than about 50 msec's worth of speech (Weinstein, 1983). (Retransmissions are impractical for interactive voice because of the propagation delays.) A recently published TDMA radio protocol (Dunlop et al., 1995) uses packets that represent 10 msec's worth of speech.

The impact of slot size on data transmissions involves another set of trade-offs:

- Packet size cannot be made too small without sacrificing throughput, since the per-packet overhead of header information and error detection is essentially independent of packet length.

- Many hybrid DAMA protocols handle single-slot data transmissions and longer transmissions differently. A longer transmission may incur call setup and teardown delays and overhead and will at least incur a setup delay, as in Li and Yan's protocol (see subsection 5.2).

- The previous two considerations seem to indicate that it is advisable to make the slots as long as possible. However, when a packet occupies only a fraction of a slot, the remainder of that slot is wasted; this implies a loss of throughput. Thus, if a high percentage of the short messages have a characteristic length, it is advisable to make the slot size just large enough to accommodate packets of this length when this does not conflict with the requirements of the voice traffic.

Although rough throughput and delay calculations can be performed analytically, selection of the optimal slot size typically requires simulation.

28

3. Protocols for the Orderwire (Request Channel)

3.1 Terminology and Concepts

Regardless of whether control is distributed or centralized, any DAMA system must have one or more channels (FDMA/DAMA) or slots (TDMA/DAMA) that are used for exchanging control information (circuit requests, assignments, and other status information). These channels or slots, together with the access protocols that govern their use, are referred to as the *orderwire*.

In systems with centralized control, the orderwire consists of a FOW for transmissions from the controller and a ROW for transmissions to the controller. In systems with fully distributed control, i.e., where users make their own circuit assignments, users announce the assignments that they have made (so that other users will not transmit on the same channels); however, we will still speak of a "circuit request" or "request." In fully distributed systems, there is no return orderwire, and the term *common signaling channel* (Edelson and Werth, 1972) is sometimes used instead of *orderwire*.

A wide variety of access schemes have been proposed for use in multiple-access communications networks. Part of the reason for this plethora of schemes is the wide variety of possible operating environments and types of user traffic. However, for any multiple access protocol, there is a maximum average rate of Poisson[1] message arrivals, or *maximum throughput*, that can be supported.

In a typical DAMA system, we might expect a high volume of short, probably fixed-length, channel request messages. Ideally, we would like to select a ROW access protocol that can serve the highest possible throughput of user requests with the minimum possible delay. Unfortunately, these objectives conflict.

3.2 Why Contention Can Be Good

In all implemented or proposed DAMA systems, the orderwire is managed using a contention protocol such as slotted Aloha (Bertsekas and Gallager, 1992).

---

[1]See subsection A.2 for a definition of the Poisson process.

Contention protocols allow request collisions, i.e., simultaneous request transmissions that interfere with each other such that none is successfully received by the resource controller. Requests are generally protected by only an error detection code, so that even a single bit error will cause the request to be discarded. Contention protocols differ mainly in the rules for determining when users retransmit following a collision. Users' equipments can automatically determine that a collision has occurred and retransmit at a later time. In systems with centralized control, the absence of any response on the FOW indicates a collision; in fully distributed systems, the equipment would have to monitor the rebroadcast on the satellite's common signaling channel.

Since request collisions cause delay and reduce the maximum request rate that the ROW can sustain, it is tempting to conclude that contention protocols are inefficient. However, when requests are generated randomly by a large population of users with low individual request generation rates, contention protocols are the only efficient multiple access protocols. Rather than attempt a rigorous justification of this statement, we shall support it by demonstrating the unsuitability of the two most important classes of noncontention protocols—polling schemes and reservations.

In a polling scheme, a central controller polls each user in turn (the poll is a sequence of bits that identifies a specific user). A user who wishes to communicate begins transmitting (on a free channel); otherwise, the user ignores the poll. The time between polls must allow for the two-way propagation delay of the channel (and for the time to reliably sense that a transmission is in progress). Typically, most users have no need to communicate. A user who wishes to access the system may have just missed his poll, in which case he experiences a long delay. Suppose, for example, that a satellite in geosynchronous orbit serves a population of 1,000 users. Since the two-way propagation delay is approximately 250 msec,[2] the time to complete a round of polls will be at least 250 seconds. Thus, polling schemes are unsuitable for satellite multiaccess. Polling is efficient only in systems with small propagation delays and small numbers of users; it is inflexible and inefficient for large user populations or user populations in which users frequently enter or leave the system.

Consider the simple reservation scheme defined in subsection 1.4. The request channel is divided into frames, each of which begins with n minislots, where n equals the number of users in the system. The length of a minislot is largely

---

[2]Two-way delay is approximately 240 msec for terminals at the subsatellite point (the point on the surface of the earth directly below the satellite) and 270 msec for terminals at the horizon.

determined by the requirement that there be sufficient guard time so that timing errors and differences in two-way propagation time associated with geographic dispersal of the users do not cause overlapping transmissions. For a geostationary satellite with an earth-coverage beam, timing differences associated with differences in range to the satellite amount to roughly 30 msec.[3] As for the polling case, we assume a population of 1,000 users. The minimum length of a frame will be 30 seconds (as a result of the minislots); frames will be longer if some users transmit requests. Thus, the average time to set up a connection is at least 15 seconds, and the worst-case time is more than 30 seconds. This performance is better than for polling but may still be unacceptable. If delay is important, reservations are practical only in systems in which propagation delays are small (or known with great accuracy) and in which noise and interference levels are extremely low; under these conditions, minislots can be made very short.[4]

The possibility of request collisions produces some unpredictability in call setup times (i.e., occasional long call setup times), but this disadvantage of contention protocols is strongly outweighed by the substantial reduction in mean call setup time and the substantial increase in the maximum throughput (volume of requests that can be handled). Mean call setup time is reduced because users can transmit requests without waiting for a poll or for an assigned minislot.

For channels with long propagation delays, efficient contention protocols must be *slotted*, i.e., time is divided into fixed-length increments and users are required to synchronize each transmission to fit within the boundaries of a slot. With unslotted protocols, two transmissions that overlap by only a few bits at the satellite will almost certainly collide, causing both to be discarded; slotted

---

[3]A small amount of *guard time* between minislots must be provided to allow for unpredicted variations in propagation time and differences between users' clocks. There is a trade-off between the amount of overhead for guard time and the hardware costs associated with synchronization. The additional complexity associated with maintaining accurate time among a population of users is small for low to medium data rate communications; highly stable clocks may not be required so long as users can periodically update their local clock using timing signals either from the satellite or from the global positioning system (GPS).

For mobile terminals that have access to the GPS Standard Positioning Service (the less accurate GPS service that is available to everyone), it is possible to *precorrect* the timing of transmissions so that the effects of both GPS position and timing errors produce a timing error (at the satellite receiving antenna) of not more than 1 μsec 95 percent of the time (private communication from Dr. Kai-tuen Woo of the Aerospace Corporation). This assumes that terminals have accurate ephemeris parameters for the communications satellite. If GPS is not available, an alternative approach is to transmit a short, user-specific string of bits to the satellite, measure the two-way propagation delay, and divide by two. The military standards for 5 kHz and 25 kHz UHF DAMA provide a special *ROW ranging slot* in each frame for exactly this purpose; the ROW ranging slots are shared on a contention basis by users who need to measure their propagation delays to the satellite.

[4]If a user slot is much longer than a reservation minislot, reservations permit very high throughput and might therefore be attractive even when propagation delays are long if delay is relatively unimportant.

protocols reduce the incidence of collisions and are therefore more efficient than unslotted protocols. During each slot, exactly one of the following three events occurs:

- No one transmits, so the slot is empty (wasted).

- The slot contains a single successful transmission.

- Two or more transmissions collide, so that the slot is wasted.

We will designate these outcomes by "0" (empty), "1" (success), and "2" (collision). By monitoring the rebroadcast from the satellite, all users learn (after some fixed delay) which of these three events occurred. Some contention protocols require that users monitor only the rebroadcasts of their own transmissions; more sophisticated contention protocols require that all users monitor the downlink continuously.

If a user transmitted during a given slot, he knows that that slot cannot be empty. Otherwise, the determination of whether a slot is empty or nonempty is generally made by measuring average power over part or all of the slot and comparing this measure against a threshold value. For nonempty slots, the determination of whether or not a collision occurred could be made by comparing the measured average power against another (higher) threshold, but this method is not very reliable. A more reliable method uses an error detection code; when a slot is nonempty, a collision is declared if carrier or bit synchronization cannot be acquired or the error detection code fails to check.[5] The detection of a collision does not provide any information about the identities of the users who collided, or even how many users were involved, except that there must have been at least two.

In performance evaluation of contention protocols, it is common to make one of the following two assumptions:

1.   There is a finite population of n users, each of which generates new packets according to an independent stationary Poisson process with rate λ/n. (The Poisson process is defined in subsection A.2). A user whose packet was

---

[5]Since an error detection code would be applied to the entire message, the code cannot be checked unless/until the entire rebroadcast of the slot has been received. Most satellite terminals are able to transmit and receive simultaneously. For half-duplex radios, the two-way propagation delay (earth-satellite-earth) must be greater than the duration of a slot; the result of a transmission in slot k can be known (at the earliest) at the beginning of slot $k+2$; this requires that the propagation delay be exactly equal to the slot duration. Even for a full-duplex radio, the result is known only after a delay equal to the duration of the transmission (one slot) plus the propagation delay. Unless the propagation delay is very small compared with the slot size (unrealistic for a satellite system), the result will not be available until the beginning of slot k+2.

involved in a collision becomes *backlogged,* i.e., the user does not generate any
new packets until this packet is successfully transmitted. The aggregate
traffic from all of the users is a nonstationary Poisson process, i.e., a Poisson
process whose average rate varies with time.

2. There is an infinite (very large) population of users, such that the aggregate
    traffic from all is Poisson with rate λ; the cumulative rate is not reduced by
    any finite number of backlogged users.

In this report, we use the infinite population model, since this reduces the
parameter space.

Performance of slotted multiple-access protocols is generally rated in terms of
delay and maximum throughput. Throughput is conventionally expressed as the
long-term average fraction of slots that contain exactly one transmission (rather
than successful transmissions per minute or second). For all contention
protocols, delay increases with throughput, approaching a singularity at a special
value—the maximum throughput. Each multiple-access protocol has a
characteristic maximum throughput.

We now briefly discuss the two important classes of multiple-access contention
protocols and their suitability for use on a DAMA orderwire/request channel:
(1) slotted Aloha and (2) splitting protocols.

3.3 Slotted Aloha

Under conditions in which propagation delays are comparable to or greater than
durations of user transmissions, and in which a large population of users
generate packets at random times with low individual packet generation rates,
both slotted Aloha and splitting protocols are very attractive.[6] (The Aloha
network protocol was developed by Abramson at the University of Hawaii in
1970 and was used to link many low-rate terminals to a central computer). The
theoretical maximum throughput of slotted Aloha is $1/e \approx 0.368$, and reasonable
values of delay are attained even for arrival rates close to this limit.

The slotted Aloha family of protocols can be defined by two rules: (1) Any new
packets generated during a slot are transmitted during the next slot; (2) if a

---

[6]For channels in which propagation delays are much shorter than typical transmission
durations, e.g., for VHF tactical radios, a class of contention protocols known as Carrier Sense
Multiple Access can provide better performance than the satellite contention protocols discussed
here.

collision occurs in slot k, each user involved in the collision independently generates a random delay b called the *backoff* and retransmits in slot k+b.

Slotted Aloha protocols differ in the rules for generating the backoff *b*; these rules are often called the *backoff policy*. The earliest proposed forms of slotted Aloha used extremely simple backoff policies in which b was generated according to a fixed (nonadaptive) distribution. In this case, the backoff policy is completely specified by the probability mass function of the backoff *b*:

$$b_k \overset{\Delta}{=} P\{b=k\}, k=1,2,\ldots. \tag{3.1}$$

There are infinitely many possible choices for this function; Table 1 shows two of the most commonly used distributions, the uniform and the geometric, together with their means and coefficients of variation.

The parameter β of the geometric distribution can be interpreted as the probability that a backlogged user retransmits in any given slot. The parameter $N>1$ or $\beta<1$ is chosen (based on the expected level of traffic) to achieve a specified performance goal; one of the most practical performance objectives is minimum mean delay.[7] Choosing a small value of N or a large value of β reduces the mean backoff but increases the probability of repeated collisions.

The delay pdf can be estimated as follows. Ignoring delay prior to the end of the first attempted transmission of a packet, the delay pdf is given by

$$(1-P_c)\delta_k + P_c\left[(1-P_c)b_k + P_c\left[(1-P_c)(b_\bullet * b_\bullet)_k + \ldots\right]\right] \tag{3.2}$$

Table 1

Two Slotted Aloha Backoff Distributions

Distribution	Probability Mass Function	Mean μ_b	Coefficient of Variation σ_b/μ_b
Uniform	$b_k=1/N, \quad k=1,2,\ldots,N$	$(N+1)/2$	$\frac{\sqrt{3}}{3}\sqrt{\frac{N-1}{N+1}} \leq \frac{\sqrt{3}}{3} \approx 0.577$
Geometric	$b_k=\beta(1-\beta)^{k-1}, \quad k=1,2,\ldots$	$1/\beta$	$\sqrt{1-\beta}\leq 1$

[7]It might be argued that one should use an objective function of the form $E\{|\,delay\,|^p\}$ with p>1, since p=1 may fail to adequately penalize occasional large delays. In simulation studies there is no particular benefit to any particular value of p; however, in mathematical analysis, the case p=1 is sometimes the only tractable one.

where P_c is the probability that a given transmission is involved in a collision, $b_\bullet$ is the backoff distribution viewed as a function of time, and $*$ denotes convolution. Exact evaluation of Equation (3.2) is not practical, but a fairly accurate approximation can be obtained by truncating after the first few terms.

The total traffic G (new arrivals plus retransmissions) is approximately Poisson with some rate greater than the new arrival rate λ. Near the maximum throughput, $G \approx 1$, and the distribution of transmissions in a given slot is Poisson with parameter G. Consequently, the probabilities of empty, success, and collision slots are approximately $1/e$, $1/e$, and $1 - 2/e$, respectively, and the fraction of transmissions that involve a collision is $P_c = 1 - 1/e$.

According to Tanenbaum (1981) simulation studies have shown that the mean delay is sensitive to the mean backoff, but somewhat insensitive to the exact shape of the backoff distribution. However, Equation (3.2) suggests that a backoff distribution with a long tail must produce a delay distribution with a long tail, except for very low arrival rates (when the arrival rate is very small there are no collisions, and the backoff distribution consequently has no effect).

Unfortunately, any fixed (nonadaptive) backoff policy is unstable for all Poisson arrival rates $\lambda > 0$ (Raychaudhuri and Joseph, 1990). Instability can be thought of as infinite delay variance or, for user populations of finite size, as very large delay variance. A straightforward heuristic explanation of this instability can be given: For any fixed value of N or β, a collision will eventually occur that involves enough users to produce repeated collisions; during this period of repeated collisions, additional users will become backlogged, so that the pool of backlogged users tends to grow at some fraction of the arrival rate λ. For a finite user population, this situation will eventually correct itself, but such behavior is nevertheless unacceptable.

This instability defect of the simplest slotted Aloha protocols can be corrected by using an adaptive backoff policy, i.e., a policy that takes into account the number of collisions that a packet has been involved in, an estimate of the number of backlogged users, or some other function of the channel feedback history (the sequence of 0's, 1's, and 2's that summarizes the outcomes of all previous slots). A general overview of such adaptive backoff policies is given by Raychaudhuri and Joseph (1990).

The most widely used adaptive backoff policy for slotted Aloha, called *exponential backoff*, is used in the Ethernet LAN protocol. Exponential backoff is similar to the fixed, uniform backoff policy of Table 1, except that the parameter N is adapted according to the formula $N = 2^C$, where C is the number of

collisions that the current packet has been involved in. According to
Raychaudhuri and Joseph (1990), more gradual backoff policies are preferable to
exponential backoff.

*The Military Interoperability Standard for Dedicated 5 KHz and 25 KHz Satellite
Communications Channels* (one of a series of standards for UHF DAMA) specifies
a variant of exponential backoff in which N takes on the values 5, 10, 50, 100, and
250. Note that some of the steps are factors of 2, but that others are even larger
than factors of 2 (the largest is 50/10= 5). Since the exponential formula $N = A^C$
produces too rapid a backoff for A=2, exponential backoff laws with bases A
greater than 2 will be even worse. The use of this particular set of values for N
does not seem justifiable.

The pseudo-Bayesian algorithm (Bertsekas and Gallager, 1992) is a modification
of slotted Aloha that achieves better delay characteristics by (1) using a backoff
policy that reflects not only the number of collisions that the current packet has
been involved in, but also information about collisions involving other packets
and (2) delaying newly generated packets so that they do not have priority over
old packets.

Users with newly generated packets immediately become backlogged. Every
user maintains an estimate $\hat{n}$ of the number of backlogged users; this estimate is
updated using the following formula:

$$\hat{n}_{k+1} = \begin{cases} \max\{\lambda, \hat{n}_k + \lambda - 1\}, & \text{``0'' or ``1''} \\ \hat{n}_k + \lambda + (e-2)^{-1}, & \text{``2,''} \end{cases} \tag{3.3}$$

where λ is the arrival rate for new packets (presumed known). Note that the
estimated backlog increases whenever a collision involving *any packet* is
observed, regardless of which user generated that packet, and decreases
whenever an empty slot or a slot containing a single packet is observed.

In any slot, a packet is transmitted with probability $\beta = \min(1, 1/\hat{n})$, i.e., $\hat{n}$
controls the rate at which backlogged packets are retransmitted. If β were held
fixed, the pseudo-Bayesian algorithm would be similar to slotted Aloha with a
geometric backoff policy (but not identical because of the different treatment of
new packets).

Assuming that $\hat{n} = n$, the true value of the backlog, we can easily show that this
transmission probability maximizes the probability that a slot contains exactly
one packet:

$$P\{\text{exactly one}\} = \binom{n}{1} \beta (1-\beta)^{n-1} = n\beta(1-\beta)^{n-1}. \tag{3.4}$$

Let

$$\frac{d}{db}n\beta(1-\beta)^{n-1} = n\left[\beta(n-1)(1-\beta)^{n-2}(-1)+(1-\beta)^{n-1}\right]=0. \qquad (3.5)$$

This implies $\beta = 1/n$.

Note that the pseudo-Bayesian algorithm requires that each user's equipment monitors the channel on a continual basis, observing the outcome (0, 1, or 2) of each slot, whether that user has anything to send or not.

Bertsekas and Gallager (1992, pp. 285–286) derive the following approximate formula for the mean delay W_R in units of slots:

$$W_R = \frac{e-1/2}{1-\lambda e} - \frac{\left(e^\lambda-1\right)(e-1)}{\lambda\left[1-\left(e^\lambda-1\right)(e-1)\right]}. \qquad (3.6)$$

In the limit as $\lambda \to 0$, $e^\lambda - 1 = \lambda + O(\lambda^2)$ and $W_R \to 1/2$. The $1/2$ accounts for the fact that a new packet must be delayed (at least) until the start of the next slot. Note that W_R is finite for all λ less than the maximum throughput of $1/e$.

3.4 Splitting Protocols

An alternative approach to collision resolution was devised independently by J. Capetanakis and by B. S. Tsybakov and V. A. Mikhailov. The Capetanakis-Tsybakov-Mikhailov (CTM) protocol was the first of a family of related protocols called *splitting protocols or tree splitting protocols* (Capetanakis, 1979a; Capetanakis, 1979b; Bertsekas and Gallager, 1992). All of these protocols have the same general strategy for coping with collisions: Packets involved in a collision are divided randomly into two groups, and each group is then retransmitted in turn.

Although there are many variations on the splitting theme, there are three basic methods:

- Randomization. Each user involved in a collision performs the equivalent of an independent coin toss; the result of the coin toss determines whether the user retransmits immediately or waits. This is the method of the original CTM protocol.

- Division by nodal address. Each user has a unique identification number consisting of m bits; let the bit positions be numbered 0, 1, . . ., m – 1. All users involved in a collision examine the kth bit of their identification number. The user retransmits immediately if this bit is a 1 or waits if it is a zero. Users involved in the next collision examine bit k+1. When k becomes greater than m − 1, it is reset to zero. When the user population is large, this method is essentially equivalent to randomization. For a small user population, division by nodal address gives slightly better performance.

- Division by time. Users keep track of the time at which they transmitted. When a collision occurs, the appropriate time interval is subdivided, and users who transmitted during the first part of that interval retransmit first. The first-come-first-served (FCFS) splitting algorithm mentioned later in this section is a special case of this class of splitting algorithms and has a maximum throughput very close to the limit of what is presently achievable for the infinite population model.

Because of the similarities among these protocols, we will discuss only splitting by randomization in detail.

In the CTM protocol, each user involved in a collision performs the equivalent of an independent coin toss, selecting group 1 with probability P and group 2 with probability $1 - P$. Users in group 1 retransmit immediately, i.e., during the slot following the one in which the collision occurred. Users in group 2 defer retransmissions until all packets in group 1 have been successfully transmitted. If group 1 or group 2 contains more than one packet, these packets will collide again and must split as before. Even if a group contains only a single packet, that packet may still collide with a new packet. All collisions are resolved on an LCFS basis. The state of the system is equivalent to a stack. Each user who has been involved in a collision keeps track of his own level within the stack, incrementing it by 1 whenever another collision occurs, and decrementing it whenever a slot is empty or contains a successful transmission. During each slot, all packets having level zero are transmitted.

Figure 10A demonstrates the operation of the CTM protocol via a tree diagram. Each circle corresponds to one time slot; T is the set of users who transmitted during that slot. An initial collision in slot S=1 involves 3 users. Users 2 and 3 fall into group 1, which retransmits in slot S=2, producing another collision. When group 1 splits, the subgroups, which we denote as 11 and 12, retransmit in slots S=3 and S=4, respectively (group 11 is empty). Note that the set of users associated with any group is not the union of the subgroups because new users can transmit at any time (user 4, who did not participate in the original collision, transmits a packet in slot 7).

The interval of time from an initial collision until its resolution is called a collision resolution interval (CRI). The CRI includes the slot in which the initial collision occurred and all slots required to resolve collisions involving those

38

users and any new users who transmit while the original collision is being resolved. In the example of Figure 10A, the length of the CRI is 9.

The maximum throughput of this version of the CTM protocol is close to the 0.368 of slotted Aloha. Moreover, the CTM protocol is inherently stable, i.e., all moments of the delay distribution are finite for any Poisson arrival rate less than the maximum throughput. (Recall that slotted Aloha was unstable without special modifications that complicate the protocol). Further discussion of the properties of the CTM protocol can be found in Feldman (1994) and Feldman et al. (1994).

Several improvements to the original CTM protocol have been devised. We mention three of these (see Bertsekas and Gallager, 1992) for a more complete discussion).

1. First note that in Figure 10A, the collision in slot 7 involves a newly generated packet, i.e., a packet generated after the initial collision in slot 1. Requiring that all newly generated packets wait for resolution of collisions yields a substantial improvement in the maximum throughput, increasing it to approximately 0.43. This version of the CTM protocol is slightly more difficult to implement because it requires that all users continually monitor the channel, even if they have nothing to transmit, or that they delay transmitting for some reasonable observation period after turning on their equipment.

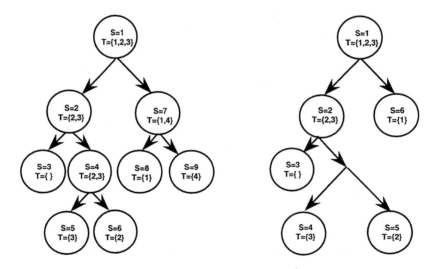

Figure 10A: Original CTM Protocol   Figure 10B: Massey's Improvement

Figure 10—Examples of Splitting Protocols in Operation

2.   Second, in the example of the CTM protocol operation shown in Figure 10A, the collision in slot 4 is unnecessary. The fact that slot 3 is empty indicates that all users who collided in slot 2 have selected group 12, i.e., are deferring their transmissions. This means that another collision is guaranteed to occur. Rather than waste a slot, the users can divide again immediately. This improvement, which is due to J. Massey, together with the first improvement mentioned above, increases the maximum throughput to approximately 0.46. Operation of the improved protocol, which we denote by CTM2, is illustrated in Figure 10B.

3.   Third, as mentioned previously, the determination of whether a slot is empty or nonempty is made by measuring average power and comparing against a threshold value. If background noise and/or interference are present, the threshold value will occasionally be exceeded even when the slot is empty. Thus, there is always some nonzero probability of falsely detecting a collision when a slot is actually empty. When this happens, the CTM2 protocol fails catastrophically because a user who generates a new packet in any slot following the false collision will wait indefinitely for the "collision" to be resolved, i.e., the CRI will be infinite. One can prevent this by imposing a maximum limit s_{max} on the number of consecutive empty slots allowed before group 2 retransmits without splitting. The original CTM corresponds to $s_{max} = 1$, while CTM2 with unlimited splitting corresponds to $s_{max} = \infty$.

One of the most attractive of the splitting protocols is the so-called FCFS splitting protocol (Bertsekas and Gallager, 1992). The maximum throughput of one variant of this protocol is 0.4878, which represents a 32 percent increase over slotted Aloha. As can be seen in Figure 11, the mean delay of FCFS splitting is less than that of slotted Aloha for any fixed Poisson arrival rate $\lambda > 0$. Slotted Aloha has been implemented far more widely than any of the splitting protocols; however, since implementation complexities are comparable and performance of FCFS splitting is substantially better, we strongly advise that FCFS splitting be considered for use in managing the orderwire in future DAMA systems.

3.5 The Number of Request Channels: One Versus Many

The classical FDMA/DAMA system described in subsection 1.3 contains 2m+1 channels; this system is capable of supporting m 2-way circuits, with the one extra channel functioning as the "request channel" or orderwire. The bandwidth of the request channel need not be the same as that of the 2m user channels.

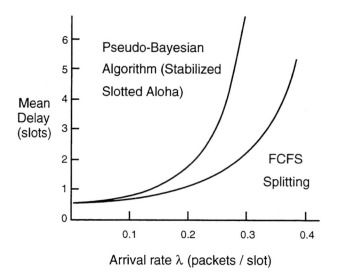

Figure 11—Comparison of Mean Delays of Slotted Aloha and of FCFS Splitting Protocols

Although a single request channel of sufficient bandwidth can in theory support any fixed call request rate, in practice it is not cost-effective to design a system with a single broadband request channel. In principle, less than 100 bits suffice to specify all of the information associated with a call request (e.g., source ID, destination ID, precedence level, and authentication); as the bandwidth of the request channel is increased, the higher data rate of the channel permits the duration of a call request to become shorter and shorter. However, assuming that the transmitter EIRP is fixed, the required receiver G/T increases in proportion to the information rate of the request channel. Thus, rather than having a single broadband request channel, it may be more practical to have several narrowband request channels. Although it is not necessary that the request channels have the same bandwidths as the user channels, making all channels have equal bandwidths is attractive because it permits one to adapt the number of request channels according to the demand on the system without changing the frequency plan.

Two other factors militate against the use of small slots. Because of errors in timing and uncertainty in the propagation delay, one must allow some fixed guard time (silence) in each slot to prevent overlapping transmissions. Efficient use of the medium requires that slots be much longer than the guard time. In addition, for a satellite in geostationary orbit, round-trip propagation delay (up to the satellite and then down again) is approximately 250 msec. Suppose that a ROW slot size of 25 msec is sufficient to accommodate timing uncertainties and the small number of bits in a circuit request.[8] Clearly, it would be wasteful to make the slot size bigger than necessary. However, the contention protocols discussed in the previous subsections seem to depend on immediate feedback. We now discuss two solutions to this problem.

Delayed Action

It turns out that most contention protocols actually can operate with delayed feedback by simply delaying action until at least part of the retransmission has been received. For slotted Aloha, this is equivalent to using a shifted backoff distribution:

$$b'_k = \begin{cases} b_{k-d+1}, & k \geq d \\ 0, & otherwise, \end{cases}$$

where $d \geq 1$ is the feedback delay in units of slots.

Shifting the backoff distribution has no effect on the maximum throughput that the protocol can support. How is the delay affected? Under a light load (G is small), there are few collisions, and consequently the delay distribution remains unchanged. Under a heavier load, the shifted backoff will increase the delay. The delay pdf can be obtained by substituting b' or b in Equation (3.2).

Delayed action does not work for splitting protocols because a user cannot determine which group he belongs to until d slot times have elapsed.

Subdivision of the ROW

An alternative approach permits efficient use of splitting protocols on satellite channels. One can divide the ROW into several subchannels using either TDMA or FDMA. The number of subchannels is chosen to make the slot size in a single subchannel comparable to the round-trip propagation delay. Consider, for example, a case in which the round-trip propagation delay is 250 msec and the slot size without subdivision is 25 msec. 10 is clearly the appropriate number of subchannels. With TDMA, slots i+j, i+j+10, i+j+20, . . . , belong to the jth subchannel, where j= 0, 1, . . . , 9.

For splitting protocols, users must maintain a separate stack for each subchannel. (If the ROW multiple-access protocol is the pseudo-Bayesian algorithm, it would be necessary to maintain a separate estimate of $\hat{n}$ for each subchannel.) The use

---

[8]In an FDMA/DAMA system, slot sizes in ROW and user channels can be different.

of TDMA subchannels for slotted Aloha is equivalent to using only backoffs that are integer multiples of the number of subchannels.[9] Thus, delayed action is preferable for protocols such as slotted Aloha.

In a DAMA system with k request (ROW) channels and $k\ell$ subchannels, a user who transmits a new request might select one of the $k\ell$ subchannels at random. However, it might be impractical to monitor all k channels at once. One possible alternative is the following: At the time the user's equipment is turned on, it randomly selects one of the k request channels and subsequently monitors and uses only this channel. When transmitting a new packet, the user's equipment might select one of the ℓ subchannels at random; delay is smaller if it uses the next available subchannel. Any requests lost because of collisions would be retransmitted via the same subchannel used for the original transmission. This approach permits one to use any of the aforementioned slotted protocols without modification.

Suppose that one could monitor all k ROW channels (this might be done, e.g., by a resource controller on the satellite that would broadcast the status of each channel via the FOW). This would permit one to modify the slotted protocols that we have discussed, e.g., to retransmit using a randomly selected request channel, with the probability of selecting any request channel a function of the estimated backlog on that channel. Intuitively, there is a potential benefit to be derived from randomizing in both frequency and time, instead of only in frequency. This idea remains to be explored.

Multiple-Channel Multiaccess Protocols

Wong and Thanawastien (1987) show that Aloha-type protocols specifically designed for operation on three parallel channels can achieve slightly higher throughputs than conventional, single-channel protocols. However, there is no benefit to using more than three channels. It is not clear that the small increase in performance is sufficient to warrant the increased complexity.

3.6 Robust ROW Access: Designing for Hostile Environments

In military systems, and perhaps in commercial systems as well, it is important that the request channels not be more vulnerable to interference and jamming

---

[9]This was pointed out to me by Dr. Joseph Han of AirTouch Communications, Inc. (private communication, September 1994).

than the communications channels. In an FDMA/DAMA system, the pattern of channel usage would make it easy for an enemy to identify the request channels. This information could then be exploited in the following manner: Since jamming of the request channels prevents users from accessing the system, and since these channels might represent only 1 to 15 percent of the total system bandwidth, a good strategy for a partial-band jammer would be to concentrate all of its power on the request channels.

In subsections 3.3 and 3.4 we discussed two important families of slotted contention protocols suitable for ROW multiple-access. The designs of these protocols were predicated on the assumption that the environment is benign; specifically, if errors are detected in a packet, the protocols assume that the errors were the result of a collision (between transmissions generated by nodes of the same network). In the presence of jamming or unintentional friendly interference, however, it might be the case that only a small fraction of bad packets (packets containing errors) are actually the result of collisions. Some contention protocols respond to collisions by forcing users to wait longer before retransmitting. For example, the pseudo-Bayesian algorithm increases the estimate of the number of backlogged users (users waiting to retransmit packets) whenever a collision is detected, and this estimate in turn controls the retransmission rate. This type of adaptation may be counterproductive when jamming or unintentional friendly interference is present.

There are a variety of ways in which DAMA systems can be modified to increase their resistance to jamming and interference; we now discuss a few of the many possible solutions.

Forward Error Correction (FEC) Coding and Interleaving

Request packets could be protected by using a strong FEC code, so that errors would be correctable with high probability. The FEC code rate might be adjusted (e.g., on command from the resource controller) to reflect changes in environmental conditions. A high-rate convolutional code (e.g., rate 8/9 or rate 3/4) or even a simple error detection code might be used under benign conditions; a lower-rate convolutional code (e.g., rate 1/3 or rate 1/4), a block code (e.g., Reed-Solomon code), or concatenated block and convolutional codes might be used under hostile conditions. For noise sources that produce long bursts of errors, interleaving might also be used.

44

Side Information for Improved Collision Determination

One could use side information, i.e., additional information extracted by analysis of the input signals prior to demodulation, to determine whether packet errors were caused by a collision between two signals with comparable amplitudes, by pulsed interference, or by a combination of the two. As an example of how such information might be used, consider the pseudo-Bayesian algorithm (see subsection 3.3). Packet errors caused by pulsed interference would necessitate retransmissions but would not be treated as collisions for the purpose of estimating the number of backlogged users (otherwise, a jammer would be able to reduce throughput not only by introducing errors into packets, but also by causing a reduction in the retransmission rate).

Spread Spectrum on the ROW

One could use frequency-hop or direct-sequence spread spectrum on the ROW. The simplest implementation would be one in which all users share a single pseudo-noise code; this is called *common code* spreading. Any protocol, e.g., slotted Aloha, that could be used with an unspread ROW could be used in the same way with the spread ROW. Alternatively, one might use an ensemble of codes, with users being divided into N groups such that members of each group share a single code. This has the advantage that only simultaneous transmissions by users in the same group produce a collision but requires greater complexity in the NCT since the NCT must now simultaneously despread and process N signals.

For any of these methods, the information rate of the request channel tends to be small compared with that of the user channels. Thus, one can achieve 10 or 20 dB of antijam protection on the request channel without the large increase in system bandwidth that would be required to provide this level of antijam protection for both request and user channels.[10]

Common-Code Spread Spectrum for the Entire System

The logical extension of the previous concept is to randomize all of the channels by frequency hopping them at a moderate rate (e.g., 200 to 20,000 hops per

---

[10]A related approach was suggested by Edward Bedrosian of RAND: If the required information rate for the request channel is small compared with the total system bandwidth, one could spread the request channel over this entire bandwidth. All user channels would experience a small increase in the background noise level.

second) using orthogonal[11] pseudo-noise hopping sequences. A simple way to do this is the following. Suppose that K frequencies are available, and that each active user is assigned a unique index from {0, 1, . . . , K – 1}; suppose that the ith user is assigned index U(i). All users synchronously generate digits from 0 to K – 1 from the same pseudo-noise sequence, producing the digit D(j) during the jth chip interval. During the jth chip interval, user i transmits using carrier frequency mod(U(i)+D(j),K). This scheme ensures that no two users transmit on the same carrier frequency during the same chip interval.

This type of common-code spectrum spreading makes it impossible for the jammer to know which channels are being used as request channels at any given time and thus forces him to jam the entire band (or most of the band) to disable the system, requiring a much higher level of jammer EIRP. The use of orthogonal hopping implies some additional hardware complexity but has little or no effect on performance.

---

[11]Some frequency hopping systems use nonorthogonal hopping sequences, which means that users transmitting with different hopping sequences produce a small amount of mutual interference. Interference increases with the number of users in the system, such that (typically) only a small fraction of the available hopping sequences can be used at any time. Nonorthogonal hopping permits reduced coordination among users, at the price of mutual interference and reduced bandwidth efficiency. Most FDMA/DAMA systems have been designed for operation in bands that are too narrow to permit the use of nonorthogonal hopping sequences.

4. Pure DAMA: Performance Results for Selected Approaches

4.1 Introduction

In this section we consider pure DAMA, i.e., DAMA protocols that make use of contention only for the ROW, and that allocate resources in a circuit-switched fashion. As noted previously, pure DAMA systems can operate efficiently when all of the traffic is voice and long data transmissions. Hybrid DAMA protocols, which can cope not only with voice and long data transmissions, but also with short data transmissions (packets), are discussed in Section 5.

To simplify the analysis, we focus mainly on the single-priority case, i.e., one in which all system users have the same priority (precedence). Defining and estimating system performance measures is easiest for this case because only one type of traffic is present.

In circuit-switched systems, call attempts (call requests) that cannot be completed immediately must either be queued or blocked (discarded).[1] Systems that block calls (e.g., the public switched telephone network) are simple to implement. Systems that queue a limited number of requests, discarding requests when the buffer is full, offer better performance when call request rates are high.

Two performance measures are of primary importance for circuit-switched systems:

1. Blocking probability. For systems that do not queue requests or that queue only a limited number of requests, this is the probability that a call attempt fails because all circuits are in use and any request queue is full.

2. Waiting time. This is the delay (for calls that are not blocked) from the moment the request is generated until the caller is notified that a circuit is available.

These performance measures reflect only the availability of the communications medium and not the quality of the link, which might be measured in terms of

---

[1]In early queueing terminology, *blocking* a call meant that it was denied immediate service, but did not necessarily mean that the request was discarded. A discarded request was said to be *cleared*. These conflicting sets of terms occasionally cause confusion.

E_b / N_0 bit error rate (BER) or symbol error rate (SER), or alternatively, in terms of a speech intelligibility measure such as the diagnostic rhyme test. See Appendix A for a brief overview of queueing system performance measures.

4.2 Typical Assumptions for Analysis of Circuit-Switched Networks

In this subsection, we present a set of typical (commonly used) assumptions that facilitate the mathematical analysis of circuit-switched communications systems[2] and discuss some of the limitations of these assumptions.[3] We have delimited each assumption by quotes to separate it from the discussion that follows. These assumptions are often used in the literature without being explicitly stated. Some of these assumptions are inappropriate for certain types of analyses.

1. "New call attempts occur according to a stationary Poisson process." It is well known (Bertsekas and Gallager, 1992) that under fairly general conditions, a large population of users generating call attempts randomly and independently produce an aggregate traffic that can be modeled as a stationary Poisson process over any short period of time. This means that interarrival times (times between successive call attempts) are i.i.d. exponential random variables. A stationary Poisson process is characterized by a single parameter, the intensity λ. λ can be interpreted as the average number of arrivals (new call attempts) per unit time.

   In analytical (mathematical) performance evaluation of communications systems, using a stationary Poisson process to model new call attempts is extremely convenient and is, in many cases, a necessity since the analysis is often intractable without this assumption. Under conditions in which this assumption is violated, it is typically necessary to use simulation to estimate performance measures of interest. We list a few conditions under which the stationary Poisson assumption tends to break down:

   a. The user population is fairly small (say, less than 20), or alternatively, a fairly small number of users account for most of the traffic in the system.

---

[2]In more complex circuit-switched systems, in which there may be multiple routes between a given pair of nodes, one must specify how a route is chosen. Because there is a unique two-hop route (up to the satellite and then down) between any pair of nodes in a simple satellite DAMA network, assumptions about route selection are not discussed here.

[3]We are not aware of any general discussion in the communications literature of assumptions for analysis of circuit-switched systems; some of these assumptions are briefly discussed in Chapter 3 of the text by Bertsekas and Gallager (1992) (the focus of that text, however, is on packet switched systems).

b. The rate of new call attempts varies with time. If one is interested in performance averages over long periods of time, e.g., several hours or an entire day, variations in the call attempt rate with time of day may be important. Alternatively, one may be interested in the transient response of the system to external events that affect all users, e.g., an earthquake or other disaster; such events can produce large fluctuations in call attempt rates. Variations in the call attempt rate can be modeled using a nonstationary Poisson process, a generalization of the stationary Poisson process (see subsection A.2). In general, replacing a nonstationary Poisson process with a stationary Poisson process having the same average arrival rate leads to optimistic assessments of system performance measures.

c. Users' transmission times are not independent. If users agree beforehand on times at which each will use the system, the interarrival times could be more regular than Poisson. If, however, nodes are coupled to sensor systems that generate messages whenever a missile launch is observed, and many sensors/nodes respond to the same launch, interarrival times will be less regular (more bursty) than Poisson. In the latter case, a modification of the Poisson process called the compound Poisson process (Grimmett and Stirzaker, 1982) may be useful.

Although there are conditions under which the stationary Poisson process is not a suitable model for call attempts, this model has broad applicability. Even when the stationary Poisson process is only an approximate model for the true arrival process, it is still useful as a basis for comparing alternative systems because ratios of queueing performance measures tend to be somewhat insensitive to small changes in traffic models.[4] Alternative arrival models will not be considered here.

2. "Call holding times are exponentially distributed with mean $1/\mu$," where μ is called the *average service rate*. This assumption, which is purely an analytical convenience, does not agree with observed statistics of real communications systems. Call holding time distributions tend to have a characteristic mode (peak value) at a positive value of holding time (the peak of the exponential is at zero) and also have tails that are heavier than the exponential (see, for example, Feldman et al., 1979). Because exponential and nonexponential distributions with equal means can produce substantially

---

[4]This may not be true if the average arrival rate is changed, especially when the normalized arrival rate ρ is close to unity (see Appendix A).

different values of mean delay and other performance measures, exponential call holding times should not be used in simulation; mathematical analyses that depend on this assumption should be qualified carefully. Under certain very specific conditions, blocking probabilities are insensitive to the shape of the call holding time distribution, i.e., they depend only on the mean call holding time. See Appendix A and Burman et al. (1984) for further discussion.

3. "Compared with call holding times, call setup (and teardown) times are sufficiently short that they can be ignored (treated as having duration zero)." This is equivalent to assuming that propagation delays are small and that collisions are rare. When call holding times are on the order of minutes and call setup times on the order of a few seconds, the effect of the call setup time on system capacity is small. Nevertheless, the reduction in system, capacity due to finite call setup times is almost always significant and must be taken into account to obtain a conservative estimate.

   It is generally reasonable to ignore call setup times when the ratio of mean call holding time to round-trip propagation delay is large (at least 10). However, when the call attempt rate approaches the capacity of the orderwire, setting up a call may involve repeated collisions on the orderwire. Each time a collision occurs, the user incurs a random delay (whose distribution depends on the particular access protocol used) and an additional propagation delay. Thus, the mean total call setup time may be much larger than a single round-trip propagation delay.

4. "Conflicting assignments occur with sufficient rarity that they can be ignored." A conflicting assignment means that the same circuit is assigned to two or more users at the same (or overlapping) times, such that interference results (as previously discussed, this is only possible in systems with distributed control). Let the total one-way propagation delay (earth-satellite-earth) be τ seconds. A circuit assignment made at time t is received by all other terminals at time t+τ. Thus, conflicting assignments occur only if one or more of the other terminals assigns itself the same channel during the interval [t,t+τ]. This is unlikely if, as is typically the case, the average time between new calls per circuit (m / λ) is large compared with the propagation delay τ.[5]

5. "The probability of finding a destination busy (attempting a call to a destination already involved in a connection) is negligibly small." This

---

[5]If channel assignments are made randomly among the m channels, then assignments (when all channels are available) form a Poisson process with rate ρ.

50

would certainly be true for a large user population in which all nodes receive approximately the same number of calls per day. In practice, it is often the case that a small number of destinations receive a disproportionately large number of calls, in which case the fraction of uncompleted calls can become significant.

6. "Queueing delays on the FOW can be ignored." Since only the resource controller can transmit on the FOW, it might appear that there should never be any queueing delays. However, in a system with multiple ROW channels, several successful requests arriving in a short span of time might force the resource controller to queue assignments; in a well-designed system, these delays should occur rarely and even then be small. Note that propagation delays on the FOW should always be accounted for.

4.3 Blocking Probabilities: M/M/m/m Model and Analysis

In this subsection, we evaluate the blocking probability for a single-precedence pure DAMA system using a fairly standard but questionable analytical approach (Dill, 1972).[6] The analysis in Dill (1972) depends on all six of the assumptions in subsection 4.2, and on a seventh, possibly faulty assumption (to be explained in the next subsection). Five of these seven assumptions are "hidden," i.e., only assumptions 1 and 2 are explicitly stated. In subsequent subsections, we will refine the analysis to reduce the dependence on questionable assumptions.

With the above assumptions, the system is equivalent to an M/M/m/m queue— the so-called *m-server loss queue* (see Appendix A). The *blocking probability* P_b, i.e., the probability that a new call request does not result in a circuit assignment because all circuits are already in use, is given by

$$P_b = \frac{\left(\frac{\lambda}{\mu}\right)^m \Big/ m!}{\sum_{i=0}^{m}\left(\frac{\lambda}{\mu}\right)^i \Big/ i!} \tag{4.1}$$

and is commonly known as the Erlang-B formula; a derivation of this formula is given in subsection A.4. Equation (4.1) is also used in Dill (1972), in which the author states that this result depends on exponential call holding times

---

[6]We begin with the simplest approach to the problem to make what follows easier to understand; the discussion provided here enlarges considerably on that in Dill (1972) to make the presentation more tutorial.

(assumption 2). However, Equation (4.1) remains true even when call holding times are not exponentially distributed (see Appendix A).

Table 2 shows the dependence of P_b on the number of circuits m for two values of normalized arrival rate (traffic intensity) λ/μ: 0.5 and 5.0.

Table 2

Blocking Probabilities for Pure DAMA (M/M/m/m Queue)

Number of Circuits, m	$\lambda/\mu = 0.5$ Blocking Probability P_b	$\lambda/\mu = 5.0$ Blocking Probability P_b
1	0.333	0.833
2	0.0769	0.676
3	0.0127	0.530
4	0.00158	0.398
5	0.000158	0.285
6		0.192
7		0.121
8		0.0700
9		0.0375
10		0.0184
11		0.00829
12		0.00344
13		0.00132

The data in Table 2 illustrate the following effects:

1. For small values of λ/μ, the system must have considerable spare capacity to achieve low blocking probabilities.

    Suppose that the availability requirement is $P_b \leq 0.01$. If $\lambda/\mu = 0.5$, m = 4 circuits are needed; the ratio of system capacity (number of circuits) to normalized traffic intensity is 8. If $\lambda/\mu = 5.0$ (the normalized traffic intensity has increased by a factor of 10), m= 11 circuits are needed (less than three times as many circuits); the ratio of required system capacity to normalized traffic intensity falls from 8 to 2.2.

2. After the number of circuits m becomes large enough to make the blocking probability small, e.g., on the order of 0.01, blocking probabilities decrease rapidly with increasing m.

3. For any fixed value of blocking probability P_b, it is possible to achieve better utilization as the normalized traffic load λ/μ increases. This so-called "statistical multiplexer effect" is just another way of viewing effect 1 above.

4.4 A Possible Problem with the Model Assumptions: Reattempts

In addition to the six assumptions stated in subsection 4.2, the analysis of subsection 4.3 involves an additional, hidden assumption, namely, that blocked calls (call attempts that do not result in channel assignments) are not reattempted. This is not a reasonable model of human behavior. It would be more reasonable to expect users to make repeated attempts to access the system, with the number of attempts (typically 2 to 20) and their frequency presumably reflecting the urgency of the communication, the number of previous attempts that failed, and perhaps also personality traits of the caller. The effect of reattempts is to increase the net traffic load on the system, which in turn causes a degradation in system performance; thus, it is important to model reattempts unless blocking probabilities are very low.

There are a variety of possible models for reattempts:

1. A user never attempts a blocked call again; this is the model of subsection 4.3.

2. A user always reattempts a blocked call (persistent reattempts), with a long random delay between attempts. If the delay is long compared with the mean call interarrival time $(1/\mu)$, the aggregate traffic (new calls plus reattempts) can, under suitable conditions, be modeled as a single Poisson process (see Bertsekas and Gallager (1992) for further discussion). In this case, however, the net arrival rate (traffic intensity) λ must be adjusted appropriately to account for the blocking. Otherwise, there would not be a fair basis for comparison of alternative systems, i.e., it would not be possible to compare two systems using equal new call arrival rates.

3. A user reattempts a blocked call frequently (at very short time intervals) until the call is successful. As soon as a channel becomes available (due to a call termination), all blocked users have an equal chance of grabbing that channel.

4. A user reattempts a blocked call, with the maximum number of reattempts (before the user gives up) determined by an arbitrary (discrete) probability mass function, and with the time between attempts determined by an arbitrary (continuous) probability density function.

The following three figures illustrate the different models. Figure 12 corresponds to model 1, the model without reattempt. Figure 13 corresponds to any of the models 2, 3, and 4. Figure 14 illustrates blocking and queueing in combination.

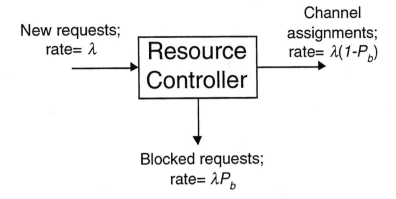

Figure 12—System With Blocking and No Reattempts

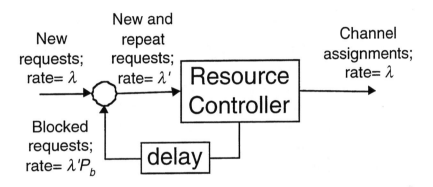

Figure 13—System With Blocking and Reattempts

Model 4 is quite general, but it is also analytically intractable. A more practical approach is to treat only models 1, 2, and 3, since these represent limiting (extreme) cases. Any distributions for number of reattempts and delay between reattempts should produce behavior that falls somewhere in between these three cases.

There is another possible method for handling blocked calls for which none of the above models are suitable. A DAMA system could be designed so that the resource controller keeps a queue of unsatisfied circuit requests and makes assignments, e.g., in FCFS or HOL priority order, as circuits become available. This approach is discussed in subsection 4.7.

54

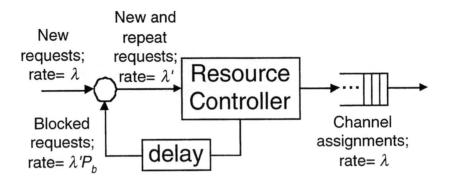

Figure 14—System With Blocking, Queueing, and Reattempts

4.5 Reattempts After Long Random Delays

In this subsection, we investigate the behavior of a single-precedence pure-DAMA system with reattempt model 2 of subsection 4.4; i.e., a user always reattempts a blocked call, with a long random delay before each reattempt. The mean delay is assumed to be much greater than the mean call interarrival time (λ/μ), and delays are assumed to be such that the aggregate traffic (new calls and reattempts together) can be modeled as a single Poisson process (see Bertsekas and Gallager (1992) for further discussion). The net arrival rate (traffic intensity), counting both new arrivals at the rate λ and reattempts, is given by

$$\lambda' = \lambda\left(1 + P_b + P_b^2 + ...\right) = \frac{\lambda}{1 - P_b},$$

(4.2)

where P_b is the probability that a specific call attempt is blocked (is unsuccessful). The Erlang-B formula Equation (4.1) still applies if we replace λ by λ'. Since λ' depends on P_b, we now have a nonlinear equation that must be solved numerically to obtain the blocking probability. As shown in Appendix B, it is straightforward to obtain a degree-m polynomial in the unknown $1 - P_b$ in a form in which the coefficients are directly available. We wrote a FORTRAN program that solves this polynomial numerically using the IMSL subroutine DZPORC.

Carrying out this calculation for the same normalized arrival rates used in subsection 4.3 yields results shown in Table 3.

The effect of reattempts on blocking probability can be seen by comparing Tables 2 and 3; the data in the rightmost columns of Tables 2 and 3 are also presented graphically in Figure 15. Figure 16 shows the dependence of blocking probability on normalized arrival rates when the number of circuits is fixed at 10.

Table 3

**Blocking Probabilities for Pure DAMA with
Persistent Reattempts**

Number of Circuits, m	$\lambda / \mu = 0.5$ Blocking Probability P_b	$\lambda / \mu = 5.0$ Blocking Probability P_b
1	0.5	1.0
2	0.0886	1.0
3	0.0131	1.0
4	0.00159	1.0
5	0.00158	1.0
6		0.428
7		0.203
8		0.0968
9		0.0453
10		0.0204
11		0.00874
12		0.00353
13		0.00134

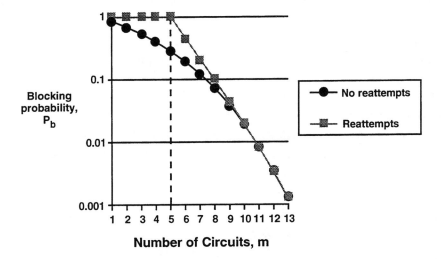

**Figure 15—Comparison of Blocking Probabilities for Pure DAMA With and
Without Reattempts for Normalized Arrival Rate $\lambda / \mu = 5.0$**

As expected, Figures 15 and 16 show that P_b is greater when blocked calls are reattempted. When the number of circuits m is much greater than the normalized new call arrival rate λ / μ, P_b is small, and there is almost no difference between the two models. However, as λ / μ approaches m, the model with reattempts exhibits a capacity-limiting effect, i.e., P_b reaches unity at this threshold. In fact, there is no solution for P_b when λ / μ exceeds m. This is a consequence of the assumption in the derivation of Equation (4.1) that the arrival

56

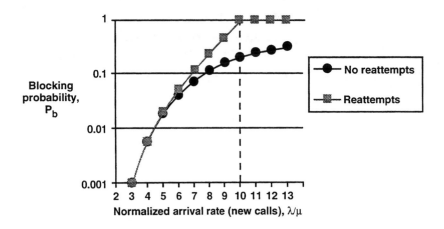

Figure 16—Comparison of Blocking Probabilities With and Without Reattempts
for Pure DAMA System with m=10 Circuits

rate λ is constant. However, when the new call arrival rate exceeds system
capacity, the summation of Equation (4.2) does not converge, and the cumulative
attempt rate λ' does not exist. Under these conditions, the number of
backlogged users (users who are waiting to reattempt a blocked call attempt)
increases without limit, and λ' also increases to infinity.

Among all possible (persistent) reattempt strategies, reattempts after long
random delays produce the minimum possible blocking probability P_b. Shorter
delays would allow the possibility that all circuits in use at the time of the
previous attempt are still in use, thus increasing P_b. However, for models with
reattempts, P_b is not the only performance measure of interest. For any system
with persistent reattempts, a user who tries to obtain a circuit will eventually be
assigned one (assuming P_b less than unity). Consequently, the distribution of
waiting time (from the initial attempt until the user is assigned a circuit) is of
greater practical importance than P_b. Note that the waiting time is the sum of all
of the interattempt times (zero if the initial call attempt is not blocked).

The simple reattempt model considered in this subsection involves an
unspecified interattempt distribution; however, if we assume that interattempt
times are i.i.d., then Wald's equality (Grimmett and Stirzaker, 1982) permits us to
express the mean waiting time E{W} in terms of the mean inter-attempt time
E{A}:[7]

---

[7]Equation (4.3) holds exactly only when the number of attempts and the interattempt times are
all independent; in practice, short interattempt times are likely to result in increased blocking because
all calls in progress at the time of the previous attempt are likely to still be in progress (because there
were no call terminations during the interim).

$$E\{W\} = \left(E\{\text{Number of attempts}\} - 1\right)E\{A\} = \frac{P_b E\{A\}}{1 - P_b}. \tag{4.3}$$

In practice, reattempts after long random delays are not very practical for real-time voice traffic because of the long waiting times that result. However, this model is important because it shows us the best possible P_b attainable in any pure DAMA system that does not queue requests. Note from Figure 11 that the best possible is not very good: Values of $P_b > 0.01$ are already observed even when the normalized arrival rate is only half the system capacity. Since it is not cost-effective to design systems with large amounts of spare capacity, we consider some alternatives to this model (reattempts after long random delays) in the subsections that follow.

4.6 Multiple Classes of Users: Should Resources Be Shared or Dedicated?

The focus of Section 3 is the egalitarian situation in which all users have equal priority. However, because systems with multiple classes of users are important for military and also for some commercial applications, we briefly consider this complicating factor. When there are multiple classes of users, one may wish to provide a better grade of service (reduced waiting time or reduced blocking probability) for higher-priority users. Alternatively, when demand exceeds available resources, one might also wish to ensure that each user class gets a specified share of the resources.[8] Either of these objectives can be achieved by using a DAMA resource controller that queues requests. For example, a preemptive or nonpreemptive priority queueing discipline can be used to provide reduced waiting times for higher-priority users (see Appendix A). Queueing of requests is discussed in greater detail in subsection 4.7.

In pure DAMA systems that do not queue requests or preempt (terminate a call to free the resources for another user), options for differentiating among user classes are limited. In an FDMA DAMA system, one can divide the available set of channels into subsets, assigning each subset to a specific user class. This approach, which is known as *dedicated subdivision*, is in some sense the opposite of fully shared access. Intermediate options are also available. Suppose, for example, that there are two classes of users, high (1) and low (2). If a total of 20 channels are available, one might dedicate 10 channels to class 1 and 6 channels to class 2, leaving 4 overflow channels available to users of either class.

---

[8]Because military communications systems tend to become overloaded in crisis situations, this is an important consideration for military systems.

58

Alternatively, one might specify that class-2 users may not use more than 6 channels at any given time, but that a class-1 user may be assigned any free channel.

A unified theoretical treatment of allocation schemes for nonpreemptive, nonqueueing pure DAMA is given by Aein and Kosovych (1977) and Aein (1978).[9] Their results reveal some interesting rules about the general behavior of such allocation schemes. In particular, *for any desired grade of service (maximum blocking probability), using any allocation scheme other than fully shared access reduces the maximum throughput that can be sustained*. As might be expected, dedicated subdivision is the most wasteful option. For dedicated subdivision, the throughput penalty becomes asyptotically small as the number of channels in each group increases. However, *for current and planned military DAMA systems, the numbers of channels are small enough that fully shared access offers significantly increased throughput (for fixed blocking probability) or reduced blocking probability (for fixed call-generation rates)*. According to Aein and Kosovych (1977), dedicated subdivision can increase capacity requirements by as much as 50 percent.

As a simple computational example, consider an FDMA/DAMA system with $m = 20$ channels operating at moderate load. Suppose that there are two classes of users with cumulative call generation rate $\lambda / \mu = 13$ $\left(\lambda /(m\mu) = 0.65\right)$. Under standard assumptions (e.g., no reattempts), the Erlang-B equation (see Equation (A.5)) applies. Substituting, we obtain $P_B = 0.018$. Now suppose that each user class accounts for half of the traffic, and that the 20 channels are divided into two dedicated 10-channel pools. Repeating the calculation, one finds that $P_B = 0.06$, i.e., the blocking probability has increased by more than a factor of 3.

4.7 FCFS Queueing of Requests at the Resource Controller

4.7.1 Background and Model Assumptions

Consider a DAMA system with a centralized resource controller that queues circuit requests that cannot be satisfied immediately; circuits are assigned as they become available. The military standards for 5 kHz and 25 kHz UHF DAMA (*Interoperability Standard for 5-kHz*, 1992; *Interoperability Standard for 25-kHz*, 1992) specify request queueing of this type. This approach offers two advantages. First, the order of service is determined by the resource controller. In particular,

---

[9]Aein and Kosovych use the exponential call holding time assumption because this permits the system to be modeled as a Markov chain. However, it appears that their blocking probability results do not actually depend on this assumption (see subsection A.7).

it is possible to provide service in order of priority (precedence). Equally important is that users in each priority class can be given FCFS service (as opposed to being served in a random order). This reduces the waiting time variability, as will be discussed in the next sub-subsection. Second, the request arrival rate is reduced because users do not need to reattempt blocked requests. This in turn reduces the incidence of collisions on the ROW, resulting in faster service.

In this sub-subsection we examine the performance of a pure DAMA system in which the resource controller maintains a queue of unsatisfied call requests. Several simplifying assumptions are needed to be able to apply analytical queueing results. We use assumption numbers 1, 4, 5, and 6 of subsection 4.2, but not numbers 2 (exponential call holding times) and 3 (negligible call setup and teardown times). In addition, we assume that all users have the same priority. We need this assumption because the combination of multiple servers, nonexponential service times, and priority queueing is analytically intractable. We also assume that users whose requests cannot be satisfied immediately receive service (circuit assignments) in FCFS order. Our final assumption is that there is no limit to the number of requests that can be queued; because the number of information bits per request is small, it should be practical to design a resource controller such that queue overflow will rarely occur, i.e., the cost of the buffer should be small even if the buffering takes place on board the satellite.

For a system that queues circuit requests, the two most important performance measures are the probability of queueing P_Q (the probability that a request is not satisfied immediately) and the waiting time until a circuit is assigned. Waiting time can be decomposed into the following components:

- *Request delay.* This is the delay from the moment the user activates the equipment, e.g., by taking the phone off hook, until the circuit request is received by the resource controller. The request delay can be an important component of the total waiting time, especially if a request must be retransmitted several times because of collisions.

- *Queueing delay.* This is the delay until a circuit becomes available.[10]

- *Response delay.* The controller reports via the FOW that a channel has been assigned to the user.

---

[10]In the event of request queueing, the controller would report via the FOW that the request has been queued (the controller might also report the position in the queue and/or an estimate of the queueing delay); however, this is not an additional component of delay because it takes place concurrently with the queueing delay.

Response delay is due almost entirely to propagation delay, since there is no contention on the FOW. Since response delay is essentially deterministic and is (for moderate to heavy traffic) small compared with the other components of delay, we will ignore it.

To be able to perform an analysis, we must first specify many more things about the system; we make several "design choices" (some are rather arbitrary, and we do not make any claims of optimality). First, this is an FDMA/DAMA system with k ROW channels and m user channels (k and m are fixed). Second, the satellite is geostationary, and the resource controller (NCT) is on the ground. Propagation delay (from a terminal up to the satellite and then down again) is approximately 250 msec. Third, the ROW slot size is 25 msec. Fourth, as discussed in subsection 3.5, let each ROW channel be divided into $\ell = 10$ subchannels, for a total of $k\ell$ subchannels. Last, let the ROW multiple-access protocol be the pseudo-Bayesian algorithm (this adaptive version of slotted Aloha was discussed in subsection 3.3).

4.7.2 Mean Waiting Time Analysis

We now carry out an approximate analysis for the mean waiting time W. (Readers who are more interested in performance implications than in technical details of the analysis can skip to sub-subsection 4.7.3, referring here for definitions of symbols.) Request delay and queueing delay are not necessarily independent—in fact, one expects these quantities to be positively correlated. However, we are interested only in the mean waiting time W, which is in any case given by

$$W = W_R + W_Q, \tag{4.4}$$

where W_Q is the mean request delay and $k\ell$ is the mean queueing delay after the request is received by the controller.

A formula for the mean delay of the pseudo-Bayesian algorithm, Equation (3.4), was given in subsection 3.3. However, we cannot directly apply Equation (3.4) here because with the division of the ROW into subchannels, slots are no longer contiguous in time. Except for the 1/2-slot delay (mean waiting time for the start of the next slot), all other components of delay in Equation (3.4) must be treated as having units of interslot times, which are ℓ times as long as the slots themselves. Thus, to obtain the delay in units of slots, it would appear that we can modify Equation (3.4) for a ROW with $k\ell$ subchannels as follows:

$$W_R = \frac{\ell e - 1/2}{1 - \lambda e} - \frac{\ell \cdot \left(e^\lambda - 1\right)(e-1)}{\lambda\left[1 - \left(e^\lambda - 1\right)(e-1)\right]} \tag{4.5}$$

There are, however, several problems with Equation (4.5). First, let the cumulative request arrival process be Poisson with rate λ, where units of λ are arrivals/sec. This is *not* the value of λ to be used in Equation (4.5). Assume that users select randomly among the $k\ell$ subchannels. By the disaggregation property of the Poisson process (see subsection A.2), the arrival process for each subchannel is Poisson with rate

$$\lambda' = \frac{\lambda \tau_{\text{slot}}}{k\ell}, \tag{4.6}$$

where τ_{slot}, the slot duration in seconds, is included to change to units to arrivals/slot.

Second, there is a problem in the limit as $\lambda \to 0$, $e^\lambda - 1 = \lambda + O(\lambda^2)$, and $W_R \to \ell - 1/2$. However, for small arrival rates, new packets are delayed only until the start of the next slot—an average delay of 1/2 slot. The reason for the discrepancy is that we mistakenly included the interslot time ℓ in the final, successful transmission. Therefore, we must subtract $\ell - 1$.

Third, Equation (4.5) counts only the delay to the start of the slot in which the packet is successfully transmitted. Since the resource controller cannot process a request packet until it is received in its entirety, we must add 1 slot time to the delay.

Fourth, units of W_R in Equation (4.5) are slots; to convert to seconds, we must multiply by the slot length τ_{slot}.

Lastly, the propagation delay for the last bit of the last transmission of a given packet must be included. This delay, which we denote by τ_{prop}, would be approximately $\ell \tau_{\text{slot}}$ for a controller on the ground and $\ell \tau_{\text{slot}}/2$ for a resource controller on the satellite.

With the above corrections, the equation for mean request delay becomes:

$$W_R = \tau_{\text{slot}} \cdot \left[\frac{\ell e - 1/2}{1 - \lambda' e} - \frac{\ell \cdot \left(e^{\lambda'} - 1\right)(e-1)}{\lambda'\left[1 - \left(e^{\lambda'} - 1\right)(e-1)\right]} - \ell + 2 \right] + \tau_{\text{prop}} \cdot \tag{4.7}$$

We now turn our attention to the component of waiting time due to queueing delay at the resource controller. The M/G/m queue seems at first glance to be a perfectly acceptable model for this component of the delay; it would seem to

62

depend on nothing more than the assumption that new requests are generated according to a Poisson process. However, there are two problems that force us to do a bit more work to justify this assumption:

1. Since a request must be transmitted within the boundaries of a slot, its transmission must be delayed (at least) until the start of the next slot. Thus, interarrival times are multiples of the slot durations and are no longer exponential. If slots are small, then the effect of the slots on the interarrival time distribution is minor (the additional mean delay of 1/2 slot must be accounted for, but it is included in W_R). In any case, the effect of the slots is to reduce the variability of the interarrival times, which means that ignoring this effect will result in a slightly pessimistic assessment of the queueing delay.[11]

2. In general, retransmissions destroy the Poisson nature of the arrival process. However, as discussed previously, retransmissions after long random delays (long compared with the mean interarrival time) combine with the new arrivals to produce an approximately Poisson process. The assumption that retransmissions occur after long delays is valid for nonadaptive ROW access protocols of the slotted Aloha family if the mean backoff is large (Clare and Yan, 1984); however, it is violated by the pseudo-Bayesian algorithm (it also fails to hold for the splitting protocols).

Because of problem 2, we must conclude that successful request packet arrivals to the resource controller *from any single subchannel* will not be Poisson. However, since outputs (successful requests) are independent from one subchannel to the next, we can treat the aggregation of all $k\ell$ channel outputs as Poisson if $k\ell$ is large enough (10 to 20 should be sufficient). Under equilibrium conditions, the average aggregate rate of successful requests must be the same as the rate λ at which new requests are generated.

Although exact expressions are not available for mean waiting time in an M/G/m queue, a variety of useful approximations have been developed; an approximation due to Yao (1985) is accurate and fairly simple and requires minimal computation:

$$W_Q = \frac{\pi_0}{\lambda} \cdot \frac{(m\rho)^m}{m!} \cdot \frac{\rho}{1-\rho} \cdot \frac{1}{1-\exp(r_m)}, \qquad (4.8)$$

---

[11]In subsection A.7 we discuss the effects of service time variability on queueing system performance; less variability is always better. The effect of interarrival time variability on performance is similar.

where m is the number of user channels;

$$\rho = \frac{\lambda}{m\mu} = \frac{\lambda\overline{X}}{m} \qquad (4.9)$$

is the server utilization factor (normalized arrival rate);

$$\pi_0 = \left[\left(\sum_{j=0}^{m-1} \frac{(m\rho)^j}{j!} \right) + \frac{(m\rho)^m}{m!} \cdot \frac{1}{1-\rho} + \frac{m\rho}{r_1} \left[e^{r_1/2} - e^{-r_1/2} - r_1 \right] \right]^{-1} \qquad (4.10)$$

$$r_j = -\frac{2(j\mu - \lambda)}{\lambda + j\mu c_X^2}, \quad j = 1, 2, ..., m; \qquad (4.11)$$

and c_X is the call holding time coefficient of variation (the ratio of the standard deviation to the mean; see also subsection A.7).

A small FORTRAN 77 program was written to evaluate the above equations for user-specified inputs. We now illustrate the behavior of this model with two examples.

4.7.3 Example 1: Effect of Call Holding Time Variability

Assume that there are a total of 20 channels—one request channel and $m = 19$ user channels. Let the mean call holding time $\overline{X} = 180$ sec (3 min), and the circuit request rate $\lambda = 5$ arrivals/minute = 0.08333 arrivals/seconds = 0.00208 arrivals/slot. All other parameters are as in sub-subsection 4.7.1.

With these parameter values, the mean request delay $W_R = 11.51$ slots = 288 msec. Note that this delay is barely more than the minimum possible value of $\ell + 3/2$ slots, indicating that collisions on the orderwire are extremely rare.

The server utilization $\rho = 0.7894$, a fairly high value. The queueing delay W_Q is shown in Table 4 for five values of the call holding time coefficient of variation c_X.

From Table 4, we see that W_Q grows faster than linearly with c_X, but not as fast as for the single-server (M/G/1) queue, for which W_Q is proportional to $1 + c_X^2$. Note that for the case $c_X = 3.0$, we would underestimate the mean waiting time by almost a factor of 5 if we predicted waiting time on the basis of the simpler M/M/m model (which requires $c_X = 1.0$). The P-K formula, Equation (A.9) in subsection A.7, gives the mean waiting time for the M/G/1 queue. A conservative method for accounting for the effect of nonexponential service is to "scale" using the P-K formula, i.e., to initially compute waiting time using the

64

Table 4

Dependence of Mean Queueing Delay W_Q on Call Holding Time
Coefficient of Variation c_X

c_X	1.0	1.5	2.0	2.5	3.0
W_Q (sec)	11.0	17.9	27.5	39.8	54.9

M/M/m model and then multiply by the ratio of waiting times for the M/G/1
and M/M/1 models. For the case $c_X = 3.0$, this method predicts a mean waiting
time of $11.0\left(1 + c_X^2\right) = 110$, which is too large by roughly a factor of 2. Theory
predicts that the M/G/m and M/M/m waiting time distributions should
converge as $m \to \infty$; clearly, for this relatively high utilization ($\rho \approx 0.8$), $m = 19$ is
still quite far from this limit.

4.7.4 Example 2: Congestion on the Return Orderwire

We now consider the case in which there are two types of requests—high priority
and low priority. The formulas for M/G/s mean waiting time given in sub-
subsection 4.7.2 do not permit priority queueing; however, the situation that we
consider here is degenerate in the sense that only delays of the high-priority
customers are of interest, and the queueing discipline is such that low-priority
customers do not contribute to this queueing delay (see below).

We know (see subsections 3.3 and 3.4) that a combined request rate that exceeds
the throughput of the ROW will prevent even the high-priority users from
receiving service. In this example, system parameters have been chosen to
illustrate this phenomenon.

Suppose that high-priority and low-priority requests arrive as independent
Poisson processes with rates $\lambda_h = 5$ / seconds and $\lambda_\ell = 142$ / seconds,
respectively. The combined arrival rate $\lambda = \lambda_h + \lambda_\ell$ determines the mean
request delay (the system does not differentiate between high- and low-priority
requests until they reach the resource controller).

Suppose that there are a total of 160 channels—one ROW channel and 159 user
channels. To facilitate analysis, the ROW is subdivided into 10 subchannels. (As
discussed in subsection 3.5, this is not the most efficient way to accommodate the
propagation delay, but our interest here is in the general behavior of a DAMA
system with limited capacity in both user channels and in the ROW.) Let the call
holding time have mean $\overline{X} = 30$ seconds and coefficient of variation $c_X = 2.0$.
The combined arrival rate (high- and low-priority together) corresponds to a
utilization factor $\rho \approx 27.7$ for the user channels. Since $\rho > 1$, it is clearly

impossible for the resource controller to satisfy the demand. Let us assume that the resource controller responds to this situation by either discarding all low-priority requests, or by using the preemptive abort queueing discipline described in subsection A.8. We also assume that requests that are discarded or aborted are not reattempted.

Under these assumptions, the mean queueing delay W_{Q_h} for the high-priority requests is exactly the same as if no low-priority requests were generated. Evaluating Equations (4.8) to (4.11) using $\lambda = \lambda_h = 5$ / seconds, we obtain $W_{Q_h} = 3.01$ seconds, an acceptable value. However, for purposes of computing the mean request delay, we must use the combined arrival rate $\lambda = \lambda_h + \lambda_\ell = 147$ / seconds, which gives $W_R = 644$ seconds $\approx 10\ 3/4$ minutes. Why is the delay on the ROW so large? From Equation (4.6) $\lambda' = 0.3675$—close to the 0.368 maximum throughput of the pseudo-Bayesian algorithm. Thus, the ROW access protocol is extremely close to collapse. Priority queueing does not guarantee fast response time for high-priority users because it does not prevent low-priority users from choking the ROW with requests.

When the request arrival rate begins to approach the maximum throughput of the ROW access protocol, the resource controller can prevent the ROW from collapsing in any of several ways.

One approach is to adaptively adjust the number of request channels. Note that in this example, converting one user channel into a second ROW channel reduces W_R from 644 sec to 0.661 sec. With 158 user channels instead of 159, the mean queueing delay W_{Q_h} of the high-priority users increases from 3.01 sec to 3.84 sec. The total mean waiting time $W_R + W_{Q_h}$ falls from 647 sec to 4.5 sec (a factor of more than 140). Other solutions to the problem of ROW collapse are discussed in subsection 5.5.

4.8 Frequent Reattempts

In subsection 4.7 we evaluated the performance of pure DAMA with FCFS queueing of circuit requests in the resource controller. In this subsection we briefly examine the consequences of what might appear to be a desirable simplification, namely, eliminating this queue. Clearly, we can no longer provide shorter waiting times for higher-priority users,[12] because when a circuit

---

[12]This is not strictly true. A DAMA controller could respond to an urgent high-priority request by terminating (preempting) a lower-priority call already in progress. However, for DAMA systems with no queueing of requests, there is no less drastic means for providing preferential service for particular classes of users.

66

becomes available, the next request received by the controller results in a circuit assignment (other, higher-priority users might also be trying to obtain a circuit, but the resource controller does not keep track of them).

In a system without priorities, one might think that we gain a small saving of memory in the resource controller at no real expense. However, this minor simplification entails a penalty in system performance; there are two reasons for this. First, for users who have an urgent need to communicate, there is a strong incentive to make frequent reattempts, since users who reattempt more frequently will tend to receive a circuit assignment sooner. If many users become backlogged and all reattempt at a high rate, the assumption that collisions on the orderwire can be ignored must break down (see the discussion of assumption 3 in subsection 4.2). Thus, even when a circuit becomes available, frequent reattempts cannot guarantee that channels that become available are immediately assigned to backlogged users. Second, ignoring the breakdown of assumption 3 must lead to an optimistic assessment of system performance. However, even if the orderwire does not significantly delay access to the system, performance is still inferior to that of a DAMA system with FCFS queueing of requests.

It is not difficult to see that if all users reattempt frequently and at the same rate, this is approximately the same as a system in which requests are queued and receive service in random order, i.e., if n customers are waiting at the moment a circuit becomes available, one of the n is selected at random and receives a circuit assignment (all n have an equal probability, $1/n$, of entering service, regardless of the order of arrival).

We now invoke a general property of queueing systems: *When we exclude queueing disciplines that select customers on the basis of how much service they require, mean waiting times are the same for all service disciplines* (see, e.g., Bertsekas and Gallager (1992)). In particular, mean waiting times under FCFS, LCFS (last-come-first-served), and random order of service are all the same. However, the mean-square waiting time (and its square root, the RMS waiting time) are less for FCFS than for any other service discipline, i.e., waiting times have minimum variability under FCFS.

We believe that the performance degradation due to service in random order will be minor under light-load conditions but substantial under heavy-load conditions, i.e., when the arrival rate approaches system capacity. Verifying this by mathematical analysis or by simulation and calculating performance measures using practical values of system parameters remains to be done.

5. Hybrid DAMA: Comparison of Selected Approaches

5.1 Introduction

Hybrid DAMA protocols combine circuit-switching (with contention or reservation schemes) with store-and-forward (packet) switching, or with other techniques, to efficiently accommodate traffic of multiple types, e.g., voice and data. A wide variety of hybrid DAMA schemes have been proposed; most of the papers that define these protocols do not use the term *hybrid DAMA*.

Much of the literature on DAMA is devoted to performance evaluation, either by analysis, simulation, or both. When a new protocol is published, the authors of the paper often compare performance with one or more alternative schemes. However, because assumptions about traffic and other aspects of system models vary from one analysis to the next, one could not compare a broad cross-section of different protocols without generating a substantial quantity of new performance results—something that the scope of this effort did not permit. Furthermore, such an "across-the-board" comparison would not be meaningful because specific protocols have been designed to optimize specific performance measures (or combinations of measures) for specific models (i.e., assumptions about traffic and the system).

Despite these limitations, there are some useful qualitative statements that can be made about the performance of hybrid DAMA protocols; we will concentrate on three specific types of hybrid DAMA that are of practical importance and can also serve as examples to explain the concepts. We also briefly discuss the analytical assumptions and methods that have been used to study the behaviors of these protocols. For detailed performance results for the protocols, the reader is referred to Li and Yan (1984); Wieselthier and Ephremides (1980, 1995); and Celandroni and Ferro (1991).

5.2 FDMA/DAMA with "Movable Boundaries" and Scheduled Data Transmissions

Pure FDMA/DAMA can be used for traffic that involves a mixture of voice and data (short messages and longer transmissions such as file transfers and faxes).

When, however, the fraction of short messages is substantial and the typical length of a short message is comparable to or less than the earth-satellite-earth propagation time, the overhead associated with the short messages may significantly reduce throughput. For example, if the average length of a transmission $\overline{L}$ is 1 sec, and average setup time $\overline{S}$ and teardown time $\overline{T}$ are each 0.3 sec, then throughput cannot exceed a fraction $\overline{L}/(\overline{L}+\overline{S}+\overline{T}) = 0.625$ of the available capacity.

A second undesirable effect is that short messages will be blocked when all channels are in use (for a controller that does not queue requests) or will occasionally experience long delays (when all channels are being used for voice calls). The available channels could be divided into separate pools for voice and short messages (see subsection 4.6). However, this would only ensure that short messages do not wait for voice call completions and would tend to increase mean queueing delays for both classes of traffic (for a resource controller that queues requests). Furthermore, it might not be clear how to divide the available channels to achieve the best long-term average performance. In what follows, *data* will be understood to refer only to short messages unless qualified.

A paper by Li and Yan (1984) improves on the concept of the previous paragraph without much increase in complexity. The resource controller does not store requests, although data requests are queued, as we explain below. Two features of the protocol are of particular interest.

First, it is reasonable to expect that the fractions of voice and data, as well as overall system utilization, will vary slowly with time. Thus, it makes sense to let the resource controller adaptively adjust the numbers of request, voice, and data channels (N_R, N_V, and N_D, respectively) according to demand using two movable boundaries, as illustrated in Figure 17. Li and Yan (1984) do this by estimating at time t the current arrival rates for voice and data requests based on successful requests arriving in the interval $[t - \tau, t]$, where τ is a design parameter.[1,2] N_R, N_V, and N_D are then selected to minimize the voice call blocking probability subject to a constraint on the total mean delay (request delay plus queueing delay) for data transmissions.

---

[1]If time scales of the traffic rate variations are slow, then τ can be increased, since this will reduce the variance of the estimate. Li and Yan do not explore how the parameter τ should be chosen.

[2]We believe that other arrival rate estimation techniques (e.g., exponential smoothing) are superior to the simple observed average arrival rate in an interval.

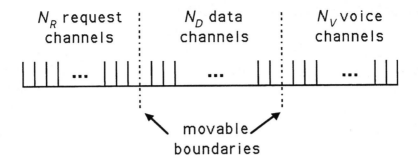

Figure 17—Frequency Plan for Modified FDMA/DAMA Protocol

Second, each data request must specify the length of the message to be transmitted; this permits scheduling of data transmissions. Since the duration of a data transmission equals the length (including header, authentication, and synchronization bits) divided by the information rate of the channel, the controller knows the remaining backlog ("work in queue") for each data channel and can thus respond to an incoming data request by scheduling it for the data channel with the smallest backlog, and by authorizing transmission to begin at a specified time on that channel. (In conventional DAMA systems, the controller specifies the channel on which a user is to transmit, and the user begins transmitting immediately upon receipt of the assignment.) Scheduling means that call teardown times are eliminated for data transmissions, and that call setup times, while adding to the total delay, have no effect on the maximum data throughput that can be achieved.

Behavior / Performance Results

For systems in which the typical message lengths are comparable to or less than the sum of the setup and teardown times, but long compared with the duration of a request packet, scheduling of message transmissions can significantly increase the maximum throughput that the system can support. Mean delay is relatively insensitive to the partition at low arrival rates but becomes increasingly sensitive as arrival rates approach the capacity limit.

Analytical Methods

Although Li and Yan (1984) do not clearly state this, they have assumed that the partitions shown in Figure 17 change sufficiently slowly that steady-state methods can be applied to each group of channels. This also permits one to treat the voice and data channels separately. The stream of successful requests is approximated as a Poisson process (we used the same assumption in sub-subsection 4.7.2). Since the voice calls do not queue, the voice channels can be modeled as an M/G/m/m queue (see subsections A.5 and A.7); as discussed in subsection A.7, the shape of the call holding time distribution has no effect on the voice call blocking probability. The data channels can be modeled as an M/G/m queue. For this queueing model, exact analytical results do not exist. Li and Yan (1984) use a different (older) set of approximations from those that we present in subsection A.7. They assume a uniform data message length distribution, but results could be generated for any desired message length distribution using the same methods.

There is an extensive literature on movable boundary multiplexor models (Weinstein et al., 1980; Kwong and Leon-Garcia, 1984; Maglaris and Schwartz, 1982; Konheim and Pickholtz, 1984; and Konheim and Reiser, 1986). Depending on the form of the boundary adaptation rules, similar methods might be applied to the movable boundary protocol of Li and Yan (1984).

5.3 FDMA/DAMA with Contention

For systems in which typical messages are short enough to be comparable in length to a request packet, it is wasteful to transmit requests for the messages. Under these conditions, we can improve on the scheme presented in the previous subsection by using any slotted contention protocol for short messages; channel assignments would still be requested for voice calls and for messages that are too long to be transmitted in a single slot, with blocked calls cleared. The three-way partition of channels would be retained, but fewer request channels would be needed for the same traffic load. If the number of request channels is held fixed, then request delays will be reduced.

If, as in the previous subsection, we assume that the partition changes slowly, then this protocol does not require any new analysis. In fact, it is not really a new protocol at all, since the request and voice channels form a pure FDMA/DAMA system and are completely independent of the data channels, which constitute a pure contention system. Thus, performance results of Sections 3 and 4, respectively, apply.

A more interesting combination of FDMA/DAMA and contention is one in which data users are permitted to use not only the data channels, but free (unassigned) voice channels as well. If the slot size is smaller than the setup time for a voice call, then the data users will have no effect on the voice users, but delay for the data users will be decreased.

In a military system, one might wish to respond to very high traffic loads by reducing the numbers of voice and reservation channels and by ordering users not to request voice channels except for the most urgent (high precedence) communications. This would maximize the number of channels available for data users. Since short text messages make much more efficient use of the bandwidth than voice users, this would maximize the amount of information delivered by the network.

Analysis

Results of Section 4 apply for the voice part of the system; however, protocols and performance results of Section 3 do not apply for the data users because of the variable number of channels. In fact, it is not clear how contention protocols such as the splitting protocols would be used in a system in which a channel can "disappear" at any moment. Slotted Aloha could be adapted to this situation by stipulating that a retransmission that would have been made using a channel that has become unavailable is made using a new channel selected randomly from the set of data channels plus currently free voice channels. To facilitate analysis, we will assume that voice call durations tend to be long compared with the slot size, so that call starts and terminations occur infrequently from the perspective of the data users.

A naive delay analysis for the data users proceeds as follows. Suppose that N_D and N_V are the numbers of channels reserved for data and for voice, respectively, and that the average voice channel utilization, i.e., the long-term fraction of the time that any given voice channel is in use, is ρ_V. The "effective" number of channels available for data users is $N_D + (1-\rho_V)N_V$ (this quantity will not in general be an integer). If new messages are generated according to a Poisson process with average rate λ_D and are assigned randomly to channels, then the average arrival rate per channel is $\bar{\lambda} = \lambda_D / [N_D + (1-\rho_V)N_V]$. We have not specified which contention protocol is being used for the data transmissions; the choice of protocol and the arrival rate $\bar{\lambda}$ together determine the delay.

This analysis suffers from a serious defect: Since the number of channels varies with time, the new arrival process seen by a given channel will in fact be a nonstationary Poisson process (see subsection A.2). A general property of multiaccess protocols is that delay is greater for nonstationary Poisson arrivals than for stationary Poisson arrivals having the same average rate. Thus, the naive analysis will tend to produce an optimistic prediction of the delay.

For the version of the protocol in which data users can use free voice channels, let us make the simplifying assumption that all boundaries are fixed. Even with this simplification, this remains a very challenging queueing problem that leads to a Reimann-Hilbert boundary-value problem. A solution is given in Konheim and Reiser (1986) and Gail et al. (1994). Unfortunately, numerical evaluation of the solution to obtain the queue length distribution is nearly unstable and consequently impractical.

Accurate evaluation of the delay experienced by the data users almost certainly requires simulation, something for future study. Other interesting questions that might be investigated include the following:

- For specified system parameters such as the total number of channels, propagation delay, and traffic statistics (including the message length distribution), what is the optimal slot size and channel partition, and what is the improvement in throughput versus pure FDMA/DAMA or Li and Yan's (1984)protocol?
- Are there conditions in which a four-way partition, utilizing assignment, scheduling, and contention, would be superior to either of the two simpler methods?

5.4 TDMA/DAMA with Reservations and Contention

In a recent paper, Wieselthier and Ephremides (1995) present a protocol called wireless integrated muliple access (WIMA). This protocol is essentially a hybrid of TDMA/DAMA with reservations and contention. Like pure reservations, the WIMA protocol permits a fixed population of n users to share a single channel (see subsection 1.4 for a discussion of reservations). Note that this is quite different from the other DAMA protocols that we have considered, which impose limits on the total rate at which requests are generated and on the number of connections simultaneously active, but not on the number of users in the system. As we shall see, WIMA is substantially more complex than pure reservations, but unlike pure reservations, efficiently supports both data and real-time voice.

The WIMA frame structure, shown in Figure 18, is in some respects similar to the reservation frame structure of Figure 6. Each status slot is divided into n minislots (the minislots are not explicitly shown in Figure 18). In general, n will be much larger than L (if this were not the case, reservations would offer little benefit over static TDMA assignment).

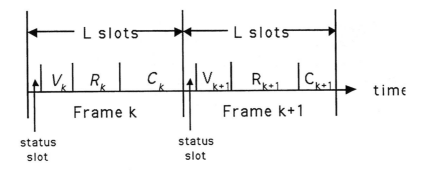

Figure 18—Frame Structure of WIMA

In addition to the status slot and R_k slots reserved for single-slot transmissions, the kth frame contains V_k slots for ongoing voice connections (one slot per connection) and C_k slots for contention. Voice users request slot assignments from the resource controller, but data users transmit in the reservation or contention slots without sending a request to the controller.

To permit real-time voice with a constant playback rate, the frame size is fixed at L slots, i.e., $1 + V_k + R_k + C_k = L$. L is also constrained by the two-way propagation delay—the status slot of frame k must be heard by all users by the end of the status slot of frame k+1. (Recall that with reservations, the number of slots in a frame varied according to the number of reservations in the previous slot.)

The concept of movable boundaries, which we discussed in subsection 5.2, can also be applied here. An upper limit V_{max} on the number of voice connections could be set by the resource controller. V_{max} might, for example, be determined from the transmission rate of the data users.

A user who generates a new data packet during frame k will transmit a reservation in his assigned minislot in the status slot of frame k+1. Because this reservation will not be heard until the end of the status slot of frame k+2, this reservation reserves a slot in frame k+2 (R_{k+2} equals the number of nonempty minislots in frame k+1). This means that delays on the order of two frame times are to be expected even under conditions of very light load.

To understand the implications of the fixed-frame length for data users, assume for the moment that there are no voice users. If the number of requests for slots in a given frame exceeds $L-1$, the excess requests must wait for the next frame (or possibly more than one frame). If the number of requests is less than $L-1$, there are extra slots that are unaccounted for. Rather than let these slots go to waste, it is sensible to allow data users to use them on a contention basis. A user who generates a packet during frame k may transmit in one of the C_k contention slots.[3] Since the success or failure will not be known until (at latest), the end of frame k+1, a user who transmits in a contention slot also requests a reservation by transmitting in the assigned minislot in frame k+1. If the contention transmission was successful, all users will be aware of this fact by the end of frame k+1 and will regard that user's reservation as "cancelled." This use of the contention slots reduces delay, especially at higher throughputs.

Analytical Methods

To facilitate analysis, Wieselthier and Ephremides (1995) consider the form of the protocol in which data users employ only reservations. A further important assumption is that call-holding times are geometrically distributed (the geometric distribution, which is the discrete analog of the exponential distribution, is the most convenient choice for a slotted protocol). These assumptions permit the network state to be modeled as a Markov chain, and the steady-state distribution of this chain can then be found by standard methods (see Appendix A). Note that the geometric distribution is a poor approximation to actual call-holding times, but other distributions cannot be explored without the use of simulation.

Behavior/Performance Results

In Wieselthier and Ephremides (1995), performance results are given for the fixed-boundary version of WIMA, i.e., the version of the protocol in which the partition parameter V_{max} (the maximum number of simultaneous voice calls) is fixed. An overall performance metric is defined as a weighted sum of blocking probability for the voice users and mean delay for the data users. Performance is more sensitive to when arrival rates are high; Li and Yan (1984) observed a similar phenomenon with their protocol (see subsection 5.2).

In general, allowing data users to transmit on unused voice channels improves system performance significantly, i.e., performance is better than would be possible for a system in which slots are dedicated for either voice or data. The degree to which delay of the data users is dependent on the voice call-holding time distribution is presently unknown. For a more realistic call-holding time distribution, the coefficient of variation (see subsection A.7) would be larger than for the geometric distribution; we conjecture that the improvement in data user

---

[3]Since these slots, unlike the reservation slots, are not associated with specific users, any transmission in a contention slot must contain a string of bits that uniquely identifies the transmitter.

delay would be less for such a call-holding time distribution (clearly, there must still be some improvement).

5.5 Preventing Row Collapse in Systems with Multiple Priorities

As demonstrated by the example of sub-subsection 4.7.4, high request rates from low-priority users can swamp the ROW, preventing high-priority users from making requests to the controller.

When the request arrival rate begins to approach the maximum throughput of the ROW access protocol, the resource controller can prevent the ROW from collapsing in any of several ways:

1. One could force users to stop transmitting low-priority or nonurgent requests, e.g., by transmitting a special command over the FOW. Under conditions of severe congestion, these requests will in any case not result in circuit assignments.

2. As discussed in sub-subsection 4.7.4, one might adaptively adjust the number of request channels, i.e., convert user channels into request channels when the request rate is high, and request channels into user channels when the request rate is low.

    In addition to the above congestion control techniques, which can be used in either pure DAMA or hybrid DAMA systems, the following techniques apply for hybrid DAMA systems only:

3. One might choose to restrict voice calls to permit a larger volume of text messages to be transmitted on a contention basis, since text messages make more efficient use of bandwidth than voice calls.

4. In a hybrid DAMA system that uses reservations and contention, reservation minislots could be provided for a small number of high-priority users. Other users would be forced to contend for the remaining (unreserved) slots in each frame.[4]

5. In a system with multiple ROW channels, one could assign one or more channels to each priority class. If these numbers were fixed, then request delays might be lower for the lower-priority users than for the higher-priority users under some conditions. Furthermore, dedicated assignment of ROW channels to specific groups of users creates the same types of

---

[4]This idea was suggested by Dr. Joseph Han of AirTouch Communications, Inc.

76

inefficiencies that resulted from dedicated assignment of user channels (recall the discussion in subsection 4.6). An adaptive version of this scheme might be workable; further research is required to work out the details and assess the benefits.

We briefly mention an approach that seems attractive but is totally unworkable. Recall the discussion of slotted Aloha in Section 3. It might seem as though using a different distribution for each class of users would permit one to control the request delays experienced by each group. However, unless the user population is small, this is not the case. Modifying the backoff distribution has no effect on the maximum arrival rate that the Aloha protocol can sustain. Permitting high-priority users to reattempt at a higher rate does not benefit them if the probability of collision is allowed to approach 100 percent.

6. Conclusions and Areas for Further Research

In this section, we present the major conclusions of this research with brief explanations, and also discuss problem areas in which the current state of knowledge is inadequate and further research is required. The material has been broken down into three major issue areas: "Architecture and Hardware Issues," "Waveform Issues," and "Protocol Issues."

6.1 Architecture and Hardware Issues

Some of the major issues for DAMA satellite system design concern the type of control (centralized, hierarchical, or distributed) and the location of the DAMA resource controller(s):

- Distributed control is attractive because there are no critical nodes in the network. However, because priority queueing of requests requires centralized or at least hierarchical control, military DAMA systems cannot use distributed control.

- As discussed in subsection 2.6, putting the resource controller onboard the satellite offers several important benefits, including reduced delay, more efficient use of resources, and switching of traffic between beams (for a satellite with a multibeam antenna). Because putting the resource controller on a ground terminal permits DAMA systems to use the existing, predominantly bent pipe transponders, it is reasonable to expect that military DAMA systems will continue to operate with ground resource controllers for at least several years. Future DAMA satellite systems should be designed with onboard resource controllers. Although no cost analysis has been done in this study, it is well-known that the costs of onboard processing and memory have fallen rapidly in the last few years. It is expected that the mix of military communications traffic will increasingly shift toward short data transmissions; this increases the performance benefits that can only be realized by using onboard resource controllers.

6.2 Waveform Issues

FDMA/DAMA Versus TDMA/DAMA

TDMA permits more flexible allocation of capacity than FDMA. For example, in a TDMA system, one might assign one slot per frame to a low-rate connection (e.g., for voice), and several slots per frame to a higher-rate connection (e.g., for video). When available bandwidth is subdivided into channels via FDMA, one may not be able to freely change the widths and locations of the channels because some satellites have fixed channelizing filters. Even for satellites that do not have channelizing filters, dynamic adaptation of the frequency plan is problematic because frequencies and power levels must be chosen to minimize intermodulation products (this is not an issue for TDMA). Also, FDMA generally requires Doppler correction.

TDMA, while providing more flexibility than conventional FDMA, is more complex to implement (users must be synchronized with the slot boundaries). More important, because users in a TDMA system transmit at low duty cycles, considerably higher transmitter peak EIRP and receiver G/T are required than for FDMA transmission for the same average data rate. Higher-peak EIRP requires a higher-power transmitter, larger antenna, or both, which in turn implies increased cost and weight. For systems that must accommodate connections requiring widely differing data rates, a combination of FDMA and TDMA is more practical than FDMA or TDMA alone (see subsection 2.2).

Vulnerability to Jamming

DAMA systems that do not protect the return orderwire are extremely vulnerable to jamming, because a jammer that concentrates its power on the return orderwire can prevent requests from reaching the controller and thereby disable the entire system. DAMA systems can be made more robust by spreading the return orderwire (via direct sequence or frequency hopping), by using a strong forward error correction code on the return orderwire, or by a combination of these approaches. Even with such protection, a jammer having power comparable to a user terminal might successfully jam selected channels but would not be able to disable the entire system. One could protect against this threat by spreading all of the channels, e.g., using orthogonal frequency hopping. Note that such hopping does not necessarily imply more than a small increase in bandwidth or power (or alternatively, a small increase in BER if bandwidth and power are held fixed). For an FDMA system with 100 channels, "randomization hopping" can provide roughly 20 dB of antijam resistance compared with any single unhopped channel.

6.3 Protocol Issues

Division of Resources: Subdivision vs. Full Sharing

Resources such as channels in an FDMA system can be divided into separate pools, with each pool dedicated to a given group of users. Alternatively, one might have a pool of channels that are reserved for high-priority (high-precedence) users. At first glance, such schemes might seem like attractive ways to guarantee that each group of users gets a "fair share" of the resources, or that high-priority users will experience lower blocking probabilities and/or delays than low-priority users.

However, subdivision has some undesirable consequences. For any desired grade of service (a maximum blocking probability), using any allocation scheme other than full sharing reduces the maximum throughput that can be sustained. For current and planned military DAMA systems, the numbers of channels are small enough that fully shared access offers significantly increased throughput (for fixed blocking probability) or reduced blocking probability (for fixed call generation rates). Dedicated subdivision can increase capacity requirements by as much as 50 percent (Aein, 1978).

Slotted Aloha Versus Splitting

Section 3 of this report covers a variety of contention protocols suitable for use on the ROW of a DAMA system. These protocols fall into two major families—"slotted Aloha" and "splitting." Existing DAMA systems use variants of slotted Aloha. It has been shown both theoretically and from simulation studies that splitting protocols, such as FCFS, could increase throughput by up to 50 percent over slotted Aloha. However, the simpler splitting protocols are vulnerable to jamming. In our opinion, modifications to these splitting protocols can address these vulnerabilities, but simulations that would confirm this claim remain to be done.

Effect of Reattempts in Pure DAMA Systems with Blocking

When the resource controller receives a request at a time when all channels are in use, the controller must do one of three things: (1) block (discard) the call, i.e., ignore the request or send a message indicating that no channels are available, (2) preempt (terminate) a lower-priority call to permit reassignment of a channel to the new call, or (3) queue the request and send a message indicating that an assignment will be made as soon as a channel becomes available.

80

Call blocking is the simplest approach. Traditional analyses of circuit-switched systems assume that users do not reattempt blocked calls. Because this assumption seems unreasonable, we decided to investigate the effects of reattempts. Results presented in subsection 4.5 show that reattempts after long, random delays result in system behavior that is very different from that of the system with no reattempts. At low new-call generation rates, reattempts have almost no effect on system performance. However, at moderate generation rates, reattempts cause a substantial increase in the blocking probability. An even more significant finding is that reattempts give rise to a "critical" new-call generation rate; as this rate is approached, the blocking probability approaches 100 percent, i.e., the system collapses.

Blocking is unsatisfactory for other reasons as well. Since blocked users will tend to reattempt calls, this increases the volume of requests on the ROW. If the volume of requests becomes too great, this can lead to overloading and collapse of the ROW, such that not even the highest-priority (highest-precedence) users can receive assignments.

Queueing of Requests in the Controller

Queueing of requests in the resource controller requires a small amount of additional memory but can offer significant performance improvements. Resource controllers that queue requests can ensure that higher-priority (higher-precedence) requests are handled before lower-priority requests, and that requests of the same priority are handled in FCFS order. While queueing of requests has no effect on the mean waiting time,[1] it reduces the waiting time variability (see subsection 4.8), an important factor for short, time-critical messages.

Handling Request Rates That Exceed Capacity

As long as the ROW does not collapse because of excessive request rates, priority queueing with preemption can be used to ensure that the higher-priority (precedence) users receive channel assignments. Preemption would be used only to reduce delays for the most time-critical calls.

---

[1]This is not strictly correct. The request delay, which is typically a small component of the total delay, is increased by reattempts. Since queueing of requests eliminates the need for reattempts, the mean request delay will be reduced.

As demonstrated in sub-subsection 4.7.4, high request rates by low-precedence users may cause the cumulative request rate to approach or exceed the maximum that the ROW can tolerate, such that even the highest precedence users cannot receive channel assignments. In subsection 5.5, a variety of potential solutions to this problem were discussed. One of the simplest of these was to include a special forward orderwire command that would force lower-precedence users to stop transmitting requests. Other techniques adapt the number of request channels or use hybrid DAMA techniques. Further work is required to define these options and to generate performance results that can be used as a basis for comparing them.

Pure DAMA Versus Hybrid DAMA

Pure DAMA protocols, including FDMA/DAMA, TDMA/DAMA, and combinations, were designed to handle voice traffic. Because of the overhead associated with call setup and teardown, pure DAMA tends to be efficient for voice calls and for long messages (e.g., file transfers and faxes), which have durations comparable to or longer than voice calls. However, pure DAMA is inefficient for short messages.

For both military and commercial mobile communications systems, the mix of voice and data traffic is changing, with short messages becoming increasingly important. The U.S. military's move to digitized forces will greatly increase the volume of short messages, e.g., for position and status reporting. Because of these changes, hybrid DAMA protocols that are capable of efficiently handling both voice and short data messages will become increasingly important.

For systems having a high volume of short messages with durations comparable to or less than the sum of the setup and teardown times, but long compared with the duration of a request packet, scheduling these short messages can significantly increase the maximum throughput that the system can support. For systems in which typical short messages are comparable in length to a request packet, there is no point in transmitting requests for short messages; it is more efficient to transmit the short messages via contention (channel assignments would still be requested for longer messages and for voice calls). In either case, adapting the numbers of channels allocated for voice, data, and requests as traffic levels vary permits one to allocate the resources where they are needed most.

Because of the potential for increased packet data throughput with given satellite resources, further attention to and investigation of hybrid DAMA are needed, with particular attention to the performance of these protocols in hostile environments.

For some military communications satellite systems that have long link acquisition times, it may be impossible to implement hybrid DAMA protocols in an efficient manner. These satellite systems may be incompatible with efficient use of DAMA. This is an important problem that requires further study.

Appendix

A. Review of Queueing Terminology, Notation, and Concepts

A.1 Introduction and Terminology

In this appendix, we define and briefly explain some of the queueing terminology and notations most commonly used in telecommunications. We also discuss some important concepts applicable to a wide range of queueing systems and present selected results from queueing theory without derivations for purposes of quantifying the phenomena. For an introduction to queueing theory (the mathematical treatment of queueing models), we recommend Bertsekas and Gallager (1992), Wolff (1989), or Kleinrock (1975).

Queueing models describe systems in which *customers* wait for some type of service, receive service, and then leave the system. In some queueing models, a customer is a human being; in others, the customer is a computer job or a part that moves through a factory. When queueing models are applied to telecommunications, the customer is a request for a circuit, a message, or a packet.

In DAMA networks, the customer is generally a request for a circuit; one must not think of the customer as a user of the system (the same user might generate many requests, each of which is a distinct customer, and a single terminal may serve many users). Service of a customer means that a circuit is assigned to the user; the service time is the same as the call-holding time.

A queueing system is characterized by the statistics of the arrival process and of the service time, by the number of servers, by the maximum queue length, and by the service discipline; we briefly explain each of these in turn.

The arrival process is typically characterized by the distribution of customer interarrival times, where an interarrival time is the difference between one arrival time and the next. Interarrival times are generally assumed to be independent.

Service times of different customers are generally assumed to be i.i.d.; however, in some models, different classes of customers have different service requirements.

In the application of queueing models to DAMA networks, the resource controller is not the server. In a simple FDMA/DAMA system, each pair of channels would be a server, assuming that a pair of channels are required to support a two-way connection. In a more complex DAMA system, one might have some customers (voice connections) that require two channels, whereas others (messages) require only one; in this situation, one must say that each channel is a server, and that some customers require two servers.

Some queues have a limit on the number of customers that can wait. In this case, an arriving customer who finds the system full departs without service; this is called *blocking*. In most queueing models, a blocked customer disappears and never returns. However, it is sometimes necessary to allow for the possibility that a blocked customer will return. The appropriate choice of model for DAMA networks is an important issue, and is addressed in Section 3 of this report.

The *service discipline* is the rule that determines the order in which a queue of waiting customers receives service; some of the more common service disciplines are FCFS, random order of service, and shortest job first. Priority queueing models are discussed in subsection A.8.

A.2 The Exponential Distribution and the Poisson Process

Exponential distributions are popular because they simplify analysis, sometimes permitting mathematical analysis when otherwise none might be possible. (In queueing simulations, however, the choice of interarrival and service distribution has no significant effect on complexity of the model, i.e., there is no incentive to use the exponential distribution in simulation work.)

Let $A(t)$ denote an arrival process, i.e., $A(t)$ counts the number of arrivals up to time t. An important special case is i.i.d. exponential interarrival times with mean $1/\lambda$; an arrival process $A(t)$ with this property is called a *stationary Poisson process of rate (intensity)* λ (we will generally omit the word "stationary"). It is well-known (Bertsekas (1992)) that under fairly general conditions, a large population of users generating call attempts randomly and independently produce an aggregate traffic that can be modeled as a stationary Poisson process over any short period of time, i.e., interarrival times are well approximated by i.i.d. exponential r.v.s. It is important to note that real-world service time distributions are rarely well approximated by the exponential distribution (see subsection A.7 for further discussion).

The Poisson process is a useful arrival model that is at least approximately satisfied in a wide range of situations (some exceptions are discussed in subsection 4.2); we do not use any other arrival model in this report.

Properties of the (Stationary) Poisson Process

The Poisson process has several important properties; we state these, providing a proof for one of the properties as an example:

1. $A(t+\tau)-A(t)$, the number of arrivals in the interval $[t,t+\tau]$, is Poisson distributed, i.e.,

$$P\{A(t+\tau)-A(t)=n\} = e^{-\lambda\tau}\frac{(\lambda\tau)}{n!}, \quad n = 0,1,....$$

2. The expected (mean) number of arrivals in an interval of length τ is $\lambda\tau$. (This follows directly from property 1.) $[A(t+\tau)-A(t)]/\tau$, the average rate of arrivals in the interval $[t,t+\tau]$ tends to λ with probability 1 as $\tau \to \infty$.

3. (Independent increments). The number of arrivals in $[t,t+\tau]$ is independent of the arrival history prior to time t; equivalently, the numbers of arrivals in nonoverlapping time intervals are independent.

4. (Aggregation). If $A(t)$ and $B(t)$ are independent Poisson processes with rates α and β, respectively, then $A(t)+B(t)$ is also Poisson with rate $\alpha+\beta$.

5. (Disaggregation). Suppose that customers arrive according to a Poisson process with rate λ. Let each new arrival go to server 1 with probability p, and to server 2 with probability $1-p$, where each decision is made independently. Then arrivals to servers 1 and 2 are independent Poisson processes with rates $p\lambda$ and $(1-p)\lambda$, respectively.

The Poisson process is often defined in terms of properties 1 and 3. We now prove that the aggregation property 4 follows from 1 and 3.

Theorem (Alternative Statement of Aggregation Property):

Let X and Y be independent Poisson r.v.s with means λ_x and λ_y, respectively. Then $Z = X+Y$ is Poisson with mean $\lambda_x + \lambda_y$.

Proof:

$$P\{Z=k\}\sum_{i=0}^{k}P\{X=i,Y=k-i\} = \sum_{i=0}^{k}\left[P\{X=i\}\{Y=k-i\}\right] =$$

$$\sum_{i=0}^{k}\frac{\lambda_x^i e^{-\lambda_x}}{i!}\frac{\lambda_y^{k-i}e^{-\lambda_y}}{(k-i)!} = e^{-(\lambda_x+\lambda_y)}\sum_{i=0}^{k}\frac{\lambda_x^i}{i!}\frac{\lambda_y^{k-i}}{(k-i)!} \quad .$$

At this point, we recognize that the final summation is similar to the binomial formula, which permits us to write:

$$P\{Z = k\} = e^{-(\lambda_x + \lambda_y)} \frac{(\lambda_x + \lambda_y)^k}{k!}.$$

The Nonstationary Poisson Process

The nonstationary Poisson process is an important generalization of the Poisson process in which the arrival rate is a function of time $\lambda(t)$. Nonstationary Poisson processes tend to provide better models for arrivals over longer periods of time and permit modeling of periodic variations in traffic, e.g., with time of day. A nonstationary Poisson process with suitable rate function can also be used to model sudden increases in traffic following an event such as an earthquake or the start of a military engagement.

Although nonstationary Poisson processes often permit much more accurate modeling of the real world, they tend to complicate or preclude analysis and are, for this reason, more useful in simulation models than in analytical models. For communications networks with queues, the existence of a steady state generally depends on stationarity of the traffic. Thus, performance measures (see subsection A.4) that are suitable for networks with stationary traffic may be meaningless with nonstationary traffic.

Because of the complications attendant on the use of nonstationary arrival models, it is tempting to replace a nonstationary Poisson process with a stationary Poisson process having the same average rate. However, for systems with any form of queueing or multiaccess protocols (see Section 3), delays and blocking probabilities are generally reduced by making such a substitution, i.e., performance results will be optimistic. For purposes of obtaining a lower bound on performance, it is usually valid to replace a nonstationary Poisson arrival process with stationary Poisson arrivals having an arrival rate equal to the maximum nonstationary arrival rate.

A.3 Queueing Notation

For "conventional" queueing systems, a convenient standard queueing notation permits one to specify most of the system characteristics in the compact format shown below:

interarrival time distribution	/	service time distribution	/	number of servers	/	maximum number in system

Table A.1

Symbols for Interarrival and Service Time Distributions

M	Memoryless (exponential)
D	Deterministic (a fixed constant)
E_k	k-Erlang (sum of k i.i.d. exponentials)
G or GI	General independent (arbitrary positive distribution)

The interarrival and service time distributions are represented by standard symbols; a few of the most commonly used symbols are shown in Table A.1.

Adjacent symbols are separated by slashes. When the queue length is unlimited, this field is omitted. For example: M/G/3/20 denotes a queue with Poisson arrivals, a general service time distribution, three servers, and a maximum of 20 customers in the system; up to $20 - 3 = 17$ customers can wait for service. The D/M/1 queue has arrivals at fixed intervals, exponential service time, a single server, and no limit on the number of customers in the system.

This notation does not specify the queueing discipline; unless otherwise indicated, this is usually assumed to be FCFS. Some unconventional queueing systems cannot be described using this notation, for example: (1) the queueing system in which some customers require one server and others require two, or (2) a queueing system in which the number of available servers varies with time (servers may break down and return to service after repair).

A.4 Queueing System Performance Measures

The formulation of a queueing model is generally an early step in a process whose ultimate goal is a planning or design decision, e.g., to compare alternative system designs to choose the better one, or to decide whether a single existing or planned system will provide the required level of performance under specified conditions. For example, in the context of DAMA networks, one might wish to know how many channels are needed to serve a population of users with specified characteristics.

Queueing models are used in making predictions of system *performance measures*. Some of the more common performance measures for queueing systems are the following:

1. *Waiting time.* This is the interval from the arrival of a customer until the start of service. In DAMA systems and circuit switched systems in general,

waiting time (the time to setup a circuit) and blocking probability (see below) are the primary performance measures of interest.

2. *System time.* This is the interval from the arrival of a customer until the completion of service, i.e., the sum of waiting time and service time. In a statistical multiplexer for packet data, the end-to-end delay for a packet (or for a message) is the primary performance measure of interest, i.e., one must count both time spent waiting in queue and the time to transmit the packet when it reaches the head of the queue (the latter is the service time).

3. *Blocking probability.* This is the probability that a customer arrives to a full queue and must leave without being served. When a user repeats a request that was blocked, this is called a *reattempt*; the question of whether a reattempt should be considered a new customer is addressed in subsection 3.4.

4. *Queueing probability.* This is the probability that a customer must wait to receive service.

5. *Server utilization or server efficiency.* This is the average fraction of the time that the servers are busy. Server utilization is of interest only for system designers—not for system users.

All of these are "steady-state" performance measures, i.e., performance measures that involve averaging over a long interval of time.

When comparing two systems, it is useful to be able to characterize the performance of each system by a single number. If mean waiting time W and blocking probability P_b are both important, one might use a weighted average to combine them into a single figure of merit F, e.g.,

$$F = \left(1 - P_b\right)W + P_b W^*,$$

where W^* is an equivalent waiting time for blocked customers (the choice of W^* depends on how much we want to penalize blocking).

Since waiting time is a distribution, a single summary statistic like the mean does not provide enough information for some purposes. For applications in which information is perishable (time critical), it is important to have information about the tail of the waiting time (or system time) distribution. One might want to know specific points on the distribution, e.g., the 50, 90, 95, and 99 percentile points. For most queueing systems, analytical methods can provide (at most) moments of the waiting and system time distributions—not the actual distributions. Given a mean and variance, it is tempting to estimate percentile points in the tail using a table for the normal distribution. However, such estimates tend to be grossly inaccurate because waiting time distributions have strong positive skewness, i.e., they are strongly skewed to the right. For some queueing models, expansions and approximations for waiting time percentiles are available; Tijms gives such an approximation for the M/G/s queue (Tijms, 1988). For most queueing models, one can obtain estimates of waiting time distributions only by simulation with careful statistical processing of the simulation outputs.[1]

In what follows, we consider only the three "standard" performance measures: mean waiting time, mean system time, and blocking probability. There is only a small class of queues for which analytical methods provide exact, closed-form expressions for these performance measures; these are queues with Poisson arrivals and exponential service times, e.g., M/M/1 and M/M/s/m.

M/G/1 is an important queueing model because it is the simplest one that accurately describes any real-world system. Note that M/M/1 and M/D/1 are special cases of M/G/1. Exact results are available for the M/G/1 queue, but they require numerical computing (numerical integration and numerical solution of systems of linear equations) except for the infinite queue limit case, where closed-form expressions are available (see subsection A.7).

There is a somewhat broader class of queues for which only approximations and bounds are available. The G/G/1 model is of this type. Of particular importance for DAMA systems is the M/G/s queueing model (it might seem that this should not be more difficult to analyze than the M/G/1 queue, but this is not the case). Useful approximations for the mean waiting time and queue length distribution are given by Boxma, Cohen, and Huffels (1979) and Yao (1985). One of two approximations for mean waiting time given by Yao is accurate to a relative error of about 3 percent (sufficient for most purposes), is fairly simple, and requires minimal computation (see subsection 3.6).

Most queueing systems are analytically intractable. In these cases, one must either make simplifying assumptions (to obtain a model that is tractable), use simulation, or do both. Simplifying assumptions that lead to a bound can be

---

[1]This is an involved subject that goes well beyond the scope of this report. Using queueing simulations to estimate distributions, e.g., of waiting time, involves several problems: (1) Outputs from a single simulation run tend to be correlated at short time lags, while conventional statistical methods require that observations be independent. (2) Initial outputs reflect initial conditions (e.g., all queues are empty) rather than the steady-state conditions of interest (the *initialization bias* problem). (3) Estimating probabilities of rare events requires long simulation runs, use of a variance reduction technique such as importance sampling, or extrapolation (a questionable practice). (4) Estimators that attempt to correct for the preceding problems are complex, and generating confidence intervals for these estimates requires the use of techniques like the bootstrap (see, e.g., Efron and Tibshirani, 1993).

90

very useful. For example, ignoring the fact that a system has a finite buffer and treating it as though the buffer were infinite may produce an upper bound on the mean waiting time for those customers who are not blocked in the finite buffer system. Such a bound might permit one to state that a proposed system will satisfy some maximum mean waiting time requirement. However, if the bound is higher than the required maximum mean waiting time, one cannot reach any conclusion. Nor could one use such bounds to decide which of two alternative systems was better.

A.5 Queues and Markov Chains

Simple queues can be represented using continuous-time Markov chains (Grimmett and Stirzaker, 1982; Bertsekas and Gallager, 1992; and Kleinrock, 1975). This representation is useful because an extensive theory for Markov chains permits us to answer a wide range of questions; in particular, we can find the distribution of the number of customers in the system, from which we can determine other quantities of interest, e.g., the mean number in the system and mean waiting time. Direct application of Markov chains is possible only for queues with both exponential interarrival times (Poisson arrivals) and exponential service times. However, indirect application of Markov chains yields useful results for some single-server queues with nonexponential service times, e.g., the M/G/1 queue. Markov chain methods are not helpful for such queueing models as M/G/s, G/G/1, and G/G/s.

The m-server Loss Queue

The state diagram of a Markov chain is shown in Figure A.1 below. This Markov chain corresponds to the M/M/m/m queue—the so-called *m-server loss queue*. This queue has m+1 possible states; the state corresponds to the number of customers presently in the system.

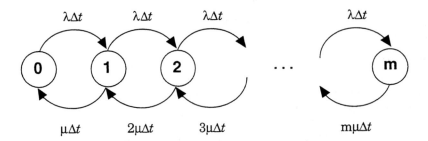

Figure A.1—Markov Chain Representation of M/M/m/m Queue

Circles indicate states; arrows indicate allowed transitions between states and are labeled with the corresponding transition probabilities. The transition probability is the conditional probability of making a transition from state i to state j in a small (infinitesimal) time interval $[t, t + \Delta t]$, given that the system is in state i at time t; this probability is approximately proportional to the length Δt of the interval.

Transitions to the right correspond to the arrival of a new customer; each arrival increases the number of customers in the system by 1, unless all m servers are already in use, in which case the new arrival has no effect (the customer is blocked). Transitions to the left correspond to the completion of a service; each service completion decreases the number of servers in use by 1. Note that the transition rates to the right are the same for all states except state m (the arrival rate does not depend on the number already in the system). However, the transition rate to the left is proportional to the number in the system (if more customers are being served, then it is reasonable that the service completion rate will be higher).

Let π_i denote the steady-state probability that the system is in state i at a randomly selected time. Under steady-state conditions, one should be able to draw a boundary at any point in the state diagram, and transitions to the left and to the right must occur with equal probability. Balance equations can be written, for example:

$$\pi_i \cdot \lambda \Delta t = \pi_{i+1} \cdot (i+1)\mu \Delta t, \quad i = 0, 1, ..., m-1 \tag{A.1}$$

from which we obtain

$$\pi_i = \frac{\rho^i}{i!} \pi_0, \quad i = 0, 1, ..., m, \tag{A.2}$$

where $\rho = \lambda / \mu$ is the *normalized arrival rate*. An additional equation can be written to express the fact that all of the state probabilities must sum to unity:

$$\sum_{i=0}^{m} \pi_i = 1 . \tag{A.3}$$

Substituting in Equation (A.3) using Equation (A.2) yields:

$$\pi_0 = \left[\sum_{i=0}^{m} \frac{\rho^i}{i!} \right]^{-1} . \tag{A.4}$$

Substituting in Equation (A.2) using Equation (A.4), we obtain the probability that all m servers are in use:

$$\pi_m = \frac{\left(\frac{\lambda}{\mu}\right)^m \Big/ m!}{\sum_{i=0}^{m}\left(\frac{\lambda}{\mu}\right)^i \Big/ i!} = P_b . \qquad (A.5)$$

The symbol P_b is used because this is also the *blocking probability*, i.e., the probability that a new call attempt finds all channels in use and cannot be assigned a channel. Equation (A.5) is commonly known as the Erlang-B formula. It has been widely applied in telephony and has also been used for estimating blocking probabilities in pure DAMA systems (see subsections 4.3 and 4.4).

Computing Steady-State Probabilites of a Markov Chain

The vector of steady-state probabilities $\pi = (\pi_1, \pi_2, \ldots)$ is important because performance measures such as delay and blocking probability are functions of the state probabilities and can often be computed immediately once π is known. For any well-behaved Markov chain, steady-state probabilities exist and can be computed by solving a system of linear equations (the balance equations). The example of the m-server loss queue led to a closed-form solution, but this is not typically the case unless the matrix of transition probabilities possesses special structure. More generally, one must solve the balance equations numerically. For Markov chains with large numbers of states, this may be impractical because the computation and storage requirements are too large.

Markov Chains with Infinite Numbers of States

For a queueing model with no queue limit (e.g., M/M/1), the corresponding Markov chain has an infinite number of states. When the average arriving traffic exceeds the average service rate of the server(s), a steady-state solution for π will not exist; this condition occurs because the queue length grows without limit, so that the steady-state probability of finding the system in any particular state is zero.

A.6 Capacity and Saturation in the M/M/1/m Queue

Let us consider the M/M/1/m queue. This is the simplest possible *finite-buffer* queueing system, i.e., a queue with both waiting and blocking. (M/M/m/m has blocking but no waiting, while M/M/1 has waiting but no blocking.) Customers arrive according to a Poisson process, are served by a single server in exponentially distributed time, and depart. If an arriving customer finds the system full, i.e., one customer in service and m – 1 waiting customers, the customer is blocked and departs without service.

This queueing model is too simple to accurately model any real-world system; the primary reason for this is that real-world queueing systems do not have exponentially distributed service times.[2] Nevertheless, the M/M/1/m queue is useful for illustrating a phenomenon common to queueing systems in general.

Let λ denote the average rate of the Poisson arrivals; the mean interarrival time is $1/\lambda$. Let $1/\mu$ denote the mean service time. We now define the *normalized arrival rate (normalized traffic intensity)*

$$\rho = \lambda/\mu. \tag{A.6}$$

A simple analysis based on continuous time Markov chains leads to the following equation for blocking probability P_b:

$$P_b = \frac{\rho^m(1-\rho)}{1-\rho^{m+1}}. \tag{A.7}$$

For finite m, Equation (A.7) is well-behaved for all values of ρ; the indeterminacy at $\rho = 1$ can be resolved by using L'Hospital's rule or by factoring the denominator using $1-\rho^{m+1} = (1-\rho)(1+\rho+\rho^2+...+\rho^m)$. From examination of Equation (A.7) we see that blocking probability tends to one of two values in the limit of increasing queue limit m:

$$\lim_{m \to \infty} P_b = \begin{cases} 0 & \rho \le 1 \\ \frac{\rho-1}{\rho}, & \rho > 1 \end{cases}. \tag{A.8}$$

Figure A.2 shows the dependence of P_b on m for selected values of ρ. Arbitrarily small P_b can be achieved when the average arrival rate λ does not exceed the maximum average service rate μ. If, however, $\lambda > \mu$ (which implies $\rho > 1$), one cannot achieve low P_b; P_b quickly approaches a nonzero limiting value with increasing queue limit m.

---

[2]M/M/1 and M/M/m queueing models are widely used in making performance predictions, but these models provide at best crude approximations to real-world queueing systems.

94

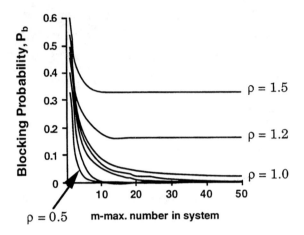

Figure A.2—Dependence of Blocking Probability P_b on Queue Limit m for Selected Values of ρ

Acceptable blocking probabilities can be achieved for any $\rho \leq 1$, but the same is not true for other performance measures, e.g., waiting time. If one examines the behavior of mean waiting time for values of ρ less than but close to unity, one finds that increasing m reduces the blocking probability but enormously increases the waiting time. In the limit of large m, mean waiting time becomes infinite as $\rho \to 1$, i.e., there is a singularity at $\rho = 1$.

A behavior similar to that of the simple M/M/1/m queue is encountered in almost all queueing systems: A queueing system has a given service capacity (maximum average service rate); when the arrival rate approaches this limit, system performance must severely degrade, i.e., changing the queue limit m permits one only to trade reduced blocking probability for increased waiting time or vice versa. It is impossible to simultaneously achieve low blocking probability and low mean waiting time unless one can restrict the normalized arrival rate ρ to hold it well below unity; a rough rule of thumb is that one should not permit ρ to exceed 0.8.

A.7 The Effect of Service-Time Variability: The M/G/1 Queue

When queueing models are applied to circuit-switched communications, the distribution of service time (call-holding time) tends to depart strongly from exponential (Feldman et al., 1979). Unlike the exponential density, whose mode (peak value) is at zero, call-holding times tend to be characterized by a positive mode. Also, the exponential distribution has too little weight in the tail (this difference, although less obvious from examination of a histogram, is particularly important for system performance).

Are these differences really important? It might seem as though one should be able to replace the actual service time distribution by an exponential distribution having the same mean value. However, making such a substitution almost always changes the resulting performance estimates—usually in the direction of overly optimistic predictions.

To quantify this effect, we consider the case of the M/G/1 queue. As previously mentioned, this model is important because it is the simplest one that accurately describes real-world systems. We cite without proof the Pollaczek-Khintchine Mean Value Theorem (P-K formula), one of the most important results in queueing theory. The P-K formula gives the mean system time T and mean waiting time W:

$$T = \overline{X} + W = \overline{X} + \frac{\lambda \overline{X^2}}{2(1-\rho)},$$
(A.9)

where

X is the service time (a random variable)

$\overline{X} = E\{X\} = \dfrac{1}{\mu}$ is the mean service time

$\overline{X^2} = E\{X^2\} = \left(\overline{X}\right)^2 + \sigma_X^2$ is the second moment of the service time

$\rho = \lambda / \mu = \lambda \overline{X}$ is called the server utilization factor.

Note that for any single-server queue with an infinite queue limit, the utilization factor ρ represents the fraction of the time that the server is busy; in queues with finite queue limits, the server is less busy because some customers are blocked and leave without service.

Equation (A.9) shows that system time and waiting time increase without bound as $\rho \rightarrow 1$. However, the P-K formula illustrates another equally important phenomenon that is more apparent in an alternative form of Equation (A.9). Making the substitutions $\overline{X^2} = \left(\overline{X}\right)^2 + \sigma_X^2$ and $\lambda = \rho / \overline{X}$, one obtains:

$$T = \overline{X} + W = \overline{X} + \frac{\rho \overline{X}}{2(1-\rho)} \cdot \left[1 + c_X^2\right],$$
(A.10)

where

$$c_X = \frac{\sigma_X}{\overline{X}}$$
(A.11)

is called the service *time coefficient of variation* and is a measure of variability. For the M/D/1 queue, service times are deterministic, which means that $c_X = 0$. For the M/M/1 queue, service times are exponentially distributed; $c_X = 1$ for the exponential. Thus, we can immediately conclude that the mean waiting time W is twice as long for M/M/1 as for M/D/1, given equal mean service times.

This phenomenon, namely, that waiting times increase with increasing service time variability, is a general property of queueing systems. For systems with a queue limit, blocking probabilities also tend to increase with service time variability (excluding systems without waiting, as discussed below). Results for the G/G/1 queue (not presented here) show that the effect of interarrival time variability is similar to that of service time variability.

Histograms given by N. E. Feldman et al. (1979) suggest that the log-normal distribution may be a good fit for call-holding time data collected for a specific system. We conjecture that $\sigma_X / \overline{X}$ lies between 1 and 3 for call-holding times in most systems; statistical testing to confirm this conjecture remains to be done. Note that with $\sigma_X / \overline{X} = 3$, one obtains mean waiting times 10 times larger than for the M/M/1 queue.

As previously mentioned, in almost all queueing systems, substituting another service time distribution (e.g., exponential) having the same mean $\overline{X}$ changes the mean delay, blocking probability, and other system performance measures. The M/G/m/m queueing system—the so-called *m-server loss queue*—is an important exception. This is the simplest reasonable model for a pure DAMA system with no queueing of requests. Service time variability does not affect the waiting time because there is no waiting in this system. Less obvious is the fact that, for M/G/m/m, the blocking probability also depends only on $\overline{X}$—other moments of the service time distribution are not important. A simple proof is given by Wolff (1989).

Consider a pure DAMA system with FCFS queueing of requests. Since each pair of channels (FDMA/DAMA with full duplex circuits) or time slot (TDMA/DAMA with simplex circuits) is a server, multiple-server queueing models must be used. Boxma, Cohen, and Huffels (1979) and Yao (1985) provide useful approximations for mean waiting time in the M/G/s queue; one set of approximation formulas given by Yao is particularly simple and is also accurate to a relative error of 3 percent (sufficient for most engineering work).

Results from Boxma, Cohen, and Huffels and from Yao show that the effect of service-time variability on waiting times is smaller for multiple-server queues than for single-server queues. In the limit of increasing number of servers, the service time coefficient of variation has no effect, i.e., only the mean service time $\overline{X}$ is important. However, for many DAMA systems, the number of servers/circuits is small enough that service time variability must be taken into account. This is particularly true for military DAMA systems because the communications satellite capacities are extremely limited, and consequently the numbers of circuits are small.

Another surprising feature of Equation (A.10) is that the mean waiting time W in the M/G/1 queue depends only on the first two moments of the service time distribution ($\overline{X}$ and $\overline{X^2}$). It turns out that this is not true for queueing systems in general. For the M/G/s queue with more than one server (s>1), W is dependent on the shape of the service time distribution; this dependence increases with increasing c_X (Tijms, 1988).

A.8 Priority Queues

In both military and commercial communications networks, it is often desirable or necessary to provide different grades of service for different classes of customers. In store-and-forward networks, one may desire shorter waiting times for control packets (packets that carry information about the status of the network), packets associated with two-way (interactive) voice connections, and (especially in military networks) packets associated with urgent messages. In a pure DAMA system or in any circuit-switched network with queueing of requests at a centralized resource controller, one may wish to provide shorter waiting times for certain categories of users, or for users whose requests indicate that the need is urgent or that the value of the information is delay sensitive (such information is sometimes said to be *perishable*). In both the store-and-forward and circuit-switched systems, we can provide smaller waiting times for higher-priority customers at the price of longer delays and/or increased blocking probabilities for lower-priority customers.

In a priority queueing system, separate performance measures for each class of customers are much more useful than simple averages over all classes. Mean waiting times for the different classes could be combined into a single figure of merit (for purposes of comparing alternative systems), but this should be done using a weighted average that reflects the time criticality of each class of customer.

For preemptive priority queueing systems, the probabilities of preemption (for each class) are important performance measures; for purposes of evaluating the quality of service that a particular class of customers receives, one may wish to add the blocking and preemption probabilities together, since in most cases a preempted service is not much better than no service at all.

There are several ways in which different grades of service can be provided; we briefly explain some of the more important approaches.[3]

1. In *head-of-line* priority queueing, also called *nonpreemptive* priority queueing, a customer with higher priority (precedence) advances ahead of any waiting customer having lower priority. Customers with equal priorities are served in order of arrival (FCFS service). A customer who has already entered service is not affected by the arrival of a higher-priority customer.

2. In *preemptive abort* priority queueing, a customer with higher priority advances ahead of any waiting customer having lower priority. If there is a lower-priority customer in service, that service is terminated. The DISA standard for SHF DAMA specifies a form of preemptive abort priority queueing in which voice users who are about to be preempted must be notified at least 30 seconds before the connection is terminated. Exact analysis of queues that use preemptive abort priority queueing is considered to be analytically intractable.

3. In preemptive resume priority queueing, a customer whose service is terminated as a result of the arrival of a higher-priority customer retains his position in the queue and resumes service after the higher-priority customer completes his service.

4. One may set aside some number of servers (circuits) for use by high-priority users. In general, this approach is attractive only when high-priority users must receive prompt service but low-priority users cannot be preempted; it is not suitable for DAMA systems.

Unfortunately, there are no convenient analytical methods for treating multiple-server priority queues with nonexponential service times (one can have any two, but not all three). Furthermore, preemptive-abort priority queues are also analytically intractable. To make some general observations about waiting times in priority queueing systems, we consider the M/G/1 queue with nonpreemptive priorities.

Suppose that there are n priority classes, with customers in class 1 having the highest priority and those in class n having the lowest priority. Assume that customers of class i arrive as an independent Poisson process with rate λ_i and that the mean and mean-square service times are $\overline{X}_i$ and $\overline{X}_i^2$, respectively.

---

[3]Part of this discussion follows the treatment in Bertsekas and Gallager (1992).

Assume that there is no queue limit $(m = \infty)$. Under these assumptions, the mean waiting time for customers of class k is given by the following formula (Bertsekas and Gallager, 1992).

$$W_k = \frac{\sum_{i=1}^{n} \lambda_i \overline{X}_i^2}{2(1-\rho_1-\cdots-\rho_{k-1})1-(1-\rho_1-\cdots-\rho_k)} \qquad (A.12)$$

As one might expect, priority queueing reduces delays for high-priority users at the expense of increased delays for low-priority users. However, priority queueing can also result in a situation in which one or more of the lower-priority classes of users receive no service at all. As

$$\sum_{i=1}^{k} \rho_i \to 1$$

from below, the mean waiting time for priority-k customers (and for any customers with lower priorities) grows to infinity, i.e., the backlog of priority-k customers waiting for service grows with time.

Although these results apply only for the M/G/1 nonpreemptive priority case, it turns out that this type of behavior is characteristic of priority queueing systems in general unless some form of congestion management is used (see subsection 2.4). For performance analysis of DAMA systems, multiple-server queueing models must be used. Unfortunately, no convenient method exists for predicting delays in a multiple-server priority queueing system. However, the conditions under which a class of users will experience long delays are essentially the same as for the single-server case: *When the total arrival rate of requests of classes k and above exceeds the system capacity, users with priorities less than or equal to k will not be served.*

The above results apply only for a system with no queue limit. For a system with a large but finite queue limit m, mean waiting times are always finite for all classes of customers. However, the quality of service for priority-k customers still degrades severely as

$$\sum_{i=1}^{k} \rho_i \to 1 \; ;$$

mean waiting times tend to become very large (for those customers who are served) and blocking probabilities approach unity; reducing the queue limit reduces mean waiting time at the cost of increased blocking.

100

B. Blocking Probability for Pure DAMA with Reattempts After Long, Random Delays

In subsection 4.5, we argued that the model for pure DAMA with reattempts after long, random delays can be analyzed like the simpler model without reattempts if the call arrival rate is modified to include the reattempts. Replacing λ in Equation (4.1) by λ' and substituting for λ' using Equation (4.2), we obtain:

$$P_b \sum_{i=0}^{m} (1-P_b)^{-i} \left(\frac{\lambda}{\mu}\right)^i \bigg/ i! = (1-P_b)^{-m} \left(\frac{\lambda}{\mu}\right)^m \bigg/ m! \ . \tag{B.1}$$

To simplify, multiply both sides by $(1-P_b)^m$ to obtain:

$$P_b \sum_{i=0}^{m} (1-P_b)^{m-i} \left(\frac{\lambda}{\mu}\right)^i \bigg/ i! = \left(\frac{\lambda}{\mu}\right)^m \bigg/ m! \ . \tag{B.2}$$

B.2 is a nonlinear equation in P_b. One approach is to solve Equation (B.2) using a general purpose root-finding algorithm for nonlinear equations. However, specialized root-finding algorithms for polynomials are more efficient than general nonlinear root-finding algorithms, and the specialized algorithms also guarantee that all roots will be found. Equation (B.2) can be viewed as a polynomial in either P_b or in $1-P_b$; the latter choice is preferable because extraction of the polynomial coefficients is easier. To obtain the coefficients, we begin by reversing the summation index in Equation (B.2).

$$P_b \sum_{i=0}^{m} (1-P_b)^i \left(\frac{\lambda}{\mu}\right)^{m-i} \bigg/ (m-i)! = \left(\frac{\lambda}{\mu}\right)^m \bigg/ m! \ . \tag{B.3}$$

The factor of P_b is now replaced by $1-(1-P_b)$ and the summation split into two summations:

$$\sum_{i=0}^{m} \frac{\left(\frac{\lambda}{\mu}\right)^{m-i}}{(m-i)!}(1-P_b)^i - \sum_{i=1}^{m+1} \frac{\left(\frac{\lambda}{\mu}\right)^{m-i+1}}{(m-i+1)!}(1-P_b)^i = \left(\frac{\lambda}{\mu}\right)^m \bigg/ m! \tag{B.4}$$

Strip off the $i = 0$ term from the first sum and the $i = m + 1$ term from the second sum and combine the remaining terms into a single sum:

$$\left(\frac{\lambda}{\mu}\right)^m \Big/ m! - \left(1 - P_b\right)^{m+1} + \sum_{i=1}^{m} \left[\frac{\left(\frac{\lambda}{\mu}\right)^{m-i}}{(m-i)!} - \frac{\left(\frac{\lambda}{\mu}\right)^{m-i+1}}{(m-i+1)!}\right]\left(1 - P_b\right)^i = \left(\frac{\lambda}{\mu}\right)^m \Big/ m!$$

(B.5)

Subtracting

$$\left(\frac{\lambda}{\mu}\right)^m \Big/ m!$$

from both sides of Equation (B.5), dividing by $1 - P_b$ (the solution $P_b = 1$ is not of interest), and changing signs, we obtain a form of the polynomial in which the coefficients are directly available:

$$\left(1 - P_b\right)^m + \sum_{i=0}^{m-1} \left[\frac{\left(\frac{\lambda}{\mu}\right)^{m-i}}{(m-i)!} - \frac{\left(\frac{\lambda}{\mu}\right)^{m-i-1}}{(m-i-1)!}\right]\left(1 - P_b\right)^i = 0 \ .$$

(B.6)

Glossary and Acronyms

Aloha   Multi-access protocol suitable for use on channels with propagation delays comparable to user transmission durations.

ARQ   Automatic repeat request. Any of several related error control schemes that involve buffering of information at the sender and retransmission of missing (failed) packet transmissions.

bent pipe satellite   A satellite that translates signals in frequency but performs no other processing. See processing satellite.

BER   Bit error rate. This is the long-term average fraction of bits that are received in error and is a measure of link quality. BER is equivalent to bit error probability.

blocking   A situation in which an attempt to establish a connection fails because of the unavailability of a circuit.

CSMA   Carrier sense multiple access

call-holding time   The duration of a call from the moment that the connection is established until the termination of the call. Although often characterized solely by the mean call-holding time, other moments of the call-holding time distribution can have an important effect on system performance measures.

call-setup time   The delay between activation of the user equipment (e.g., taking a phone off hook) until a connection is established, including propagation delays and switching and other processing delays.

call teardown time   The delay between the end of a call and when the resource controller becomes aware that the channel is free.

circuit switching	A method of communications network resource allocation in which a fixed amount of capacity is allocated on each link along the path from sender to receiver for the duration of the connection; this capacity cannot be used for any other connection during this time. See packet switching.
collision	This occurs when two users transmit in the same channel at the same time, so that their interference prevents either transmission from being received successfully.
contention protocols	Contention protocols are a broad class of multiple access protocols that permit collisions and prescribe a method for resolving the collisions.
CRI	Collision resolution interval
CTM	Capetanakis-Tsybakov-Mikhailov (coinventors of the first splitting procotol)
DAMA	Demand assignment multiple access is a loosely defined class of multiple-access techniques involving the use of circuit switching.
DISA	Defense Information Systems Agency
DS	Direct sequence, a type of spread spectrum waveform
DSCS	Defense Satellite Communications System
duplex	A communications link that permits two-way transmission is called *full-duplex* if simultaneous transmissions are possible in both directions, or *half-duplex* if transmission is possible in only one direction at a time. "Push-to-talk" radios are half-duplex. See simplex.
E_b / N_0	The ratio of signal energy per bit to one-sided noise power spectral density; also denoted by signal-to-noise ratio (SNR).
EIRP	Equivalent isotropic radiated power (previously, effective isotropic radiated power); the power (in Watts) that a hypothetical isotropic antenna would need to radiate to produce the same power density (Watts/m^2) at the receiving antenna. EIRP equals the product of radiated power and antenna gain in the given direction.
FCFS	First-come-first-served (same as FIFO)

FDMA	Frequency-division multiple access. A band of frequencies is subdivided into channels separated by guard bands. See TDMA and guard band.
FEC	Forward error correction
FH	Frequency hop, a type of spread spectrum waveform
FIFO	First-in-first-out (same as FCFS).
FOW	Forward orderwire
geo-stationary	Satellites with circular orbits having no inclination and an altitude of 35,860 km match the rotation of the earth, so that elevation and azimuth are fixed at any fixed ground terminal.
GPS	The global positioning system is a constellation of 24 satellites that provides navigation information to military and civilian users. Signals from any four satellites enable a user to determine three-space position and time. For users on the surface of the earth, three GPS satellites must be visible. GPS provides two sets of signals; the less accurate standard positioning service is available to everyone.
G/T	Antenna gain, G, divided by effective system noise temperature T; a measure of antenna and receiver system quality.
guard band	In an FDMA system, adjacent channels are separated by guard bands so that interference between signals in adjacent channels is minimized. The required guard band depends on the acceptable level of signal spillover, on how closely power is balanced between channels, on the type of modulation being used, and on channel-to-channel variation in Doppler shift.
guard time	In a TDMA system, a period of silence in each slot. There must be sufficient guard time so that timing errors (due to clock drifts and uncorrected differences in two-way propagation time) do not cause overlapping transmissions. Differences in two-way propagation are the result of geographic dispersal of the users.

106

HOL priority queueing	Head-of-line priority queueing, also called *nonpreemptive* priority queueing. A queueing discipline in which a customer with higher priority (precedence) advances ahead of any waiting customer having lower priority. Customers with equal priorities are served in order of arrival (FCFS service). A customer who has already entered service is not affected by the arrival of a higher-priority customer.
i.i.d.	Independent and identically distributed; a property of a collection of random variables.
LAN	Local area network
LCFS	Last-come-first-served (same as LIFO).
LIFO	Last-in-first-out (same as LCFS).
LOS	Line of sight. The existence of an unobstructed straight-line path between two points.
MIPS	Millions of instructions per second, a measure of computing power.
MSK	Minimum shift keying
multiple-access protocol	A distributed algorithm that controls access to a shared communications channel or channels, e.g., by specifying when a user may access a channel, what happens if the attempt fails, etc.
NCT	Network control terminal. A terminal whose primary function is to track the status of all channels under its control, grant access to users at other terminals, etc.
orderwire	One or more channels in an FDMA/DAMA system or slots in a TDMA/DAMA system reserved for the transmission of management, control, and status information to/from the resource controller.
packet switching	A method for sharing communications network resources in which information is transmitted in packets (identifiable blocks of bits) of fixed or variable length. Packets associated with any number of connections (source-sink pairs) can share the same physical links; no capacity is reserved for any specific connection. See circuit switching.

processing satellite	A satellite that, at a minimum, demodulates and remodulates the signal. (This includes despreading and spreading if spread spectrum is being used.) A full processing satellite would also decode and re-encode if error control coding is being used. Same as regenerative satellite. See bent pipe satellite.
QAM	Quadrature amplitude modulation
QPSK	Quadrature phase shift keying
RAM	Random access memory
ROW	Return orderwire
rov	random variable
SER	Symbol error rate. This is the long-term average fraction of symbols that are received in error and is a measure of link quality of BER.
service discipline	In a queueing system, the order in which a queue of waiting customers receives service; some of the more common service disciplines are first-come-first-served (FCFS), random order of service, shortest job first, and head-of-line (HOL) priority.
SFSK	Sinusoidal frequency shift keying
SHF	Super high frequency
simplex	A communications link that permits transmission in only one direction at a time is called a *simplex* link. See duplex.
slotted protocol	Time is divided into fixed-length increments; users are required to synchronize their transmissions to fit within the boundaries of a slot.
SPADE	A demand assignment multiple access (DAMA) system used with the INTELSAT IV; SPADE was the first implementation of DAMA. The acronym was derived from single-channel-per-carrier, PCM, multiple-access, demand-assignment equipment.
SRAM	Static RAM

store-and-forward	In packet-switched networks, a packet may be queued (stored in a buffer) at any node while waiting for its turn to be transmitted. A packet may wait for other packets that arrived ahead of it, for packets with higher priorities, or for the end of a link outage.
TDMA	In time-division multiple access, a channel is divided into *frames* (intervals of time) which are further sub-divided into *slots*. Each user has an assigned slot within a frame and must synchronize his transmission to fit within that slot. See FDMA.
UFO	UHF follow on
UHF	Ultra-high frequency
WIMA	Wireless integrated multiple access

References

Aein, J., and O. S. Kosovych, "Satellite capacity allocation," *Proceedings of the IEEE*, Vol. 65, No. 3, March 1977.

Aein, J. M., "A multi-user-class, blocked-calls-cleared, demand access model," *IEEE Transactions on Communications*, Vol. COM-26, No. 3, March 1978.

Bertsekas, D., and R. Gallager, *Data Networks*, Second Edition, Prentice-Hall, 1992.

Boag, J. F., "Some considerations in the design and operation of a demand assignment signaling and switching sub-system (DASSS)," *Proceedings of the INTELSAT/IEE International Conference on Digital Satellite Communications*, London, November 1969.

Boxma, O. J., J. W. Cohen, and N. Huffels, "Approximations of the mean waiting time in an M/G/s queueing system," *Operations Research*, Vol. 27, No. 6, pp. 1115–1127, November–December 1979.

Burman, D. Y., J. P. Lehoczky, and Y. Lim, "Insensitivity of blocking probabilities in a circuit-switched network," *J. of Applied Probability*, Vol. 21, pp. 850–859, 1984.

Capetanakis, J. I., "Tree algorithms for packet broadcast channels," *IEEE Trans. Inform. Theory*, Vol. IT-25, No. 5, pp. 505–515, 1979a.

Capetanakis, J. I., "Generalized TDMA: The multi-accessing tree protocol," *IEEE Trans. on Communications*, Vol. COM-27, No. 10, October 1979b.

Celandroni, N., and E. Ferro, "The FODA-TDMA satellite access scheme: presentation, study of the system, and results," *IEEE Trans. on Communications*, Vol. 39, No. 12, October 1991.

Clare, L. P., and T. Y. Yan, "The interdeparture time distribution of a pure Aloha channel with arbitrary renewal arrival process," *Proc. GLOBECOM '84*, November 1984.

Defense Information Systems Agency, *SHF Demand Assigned Multiple Access (DAMA) Standard*, Joint Interoperability and Engineering Organization, September 1993.

Dill, G. D., "Comparison of circuit call capacity of demand-assignment and preassignment operation," *COMSAT Technical Review*, Vol. 2, No. 1, 1972.

Dunlop, J., J. Irvine, D. Robertson, and P. Cosimini, "Performance of a statistically muliplexed access mechanism for a TDMA radio interface," *IEEE Personal Communications*, Vol. 2, No. 3, June 1995.

Edelson, B. I., and A. M. Werth, "SPADE system progress and application," *COMSAT Technical Review*, Vol. 2, No. 1, 1972.

Efron, B., and R. J. Tibshirani, *An Introduction to the Bootstrap*, Chapman and Hall, 1993.

Evans, B. G., ed., *Satellite Communications Systems*, 2nd Edition, Peter Peregrinus, 1991.

Fang, R. J. F., "A demand-assigned mixed TDMA and FDMA/TDMA system," *COMSAT Technical Review*, Vol. 12, No. 1, Spring 1982.

"Fast SRAMs Keep Pace with Military Applications," *Military and Aerospace Electronics*, February 1995.

Feldman, N. E., and S. J. Dudzinsky, Jr., "A New Approach to Millimeter-Wave Communications," RAND, R-1936-RC, Santa Monica, Calif., April 1977.

Feldman, N. E., W. Sollfrey, S. Katz, and S. J., Dudzinsky Jr., *Writer-to-Reader Delays in Military Communications Systems*, RAND, R-2473-AF, Santa Monica, Calif., October 1979.

Feldman, P. M., "Limiting Distribution of the Collision Resolution Interval for a Multiple Access Protocol," *Proceedings of the 1st International Conf. on Approximation, Probability, and Related Fields*, G. Anastassiou and S. T. Rachev, eds., Plenum Press, 1994.

Feldman, P. M., S. T. Rachev, and L. Rüschendorf, "Limit theorems for recursive algorithms," *J. of Computational and Applied Math.*, Vol. 56, 1994.

Gail, H. R., et al., "An analysis of a class of telecommunication models," *Performance Evaluation*, Vol. 21, pp. 151–161, 1994.

Grimmett, G., and D. Stirzaker, *Probability and Random Processes*, Oxford University Press, 1982.

Interoperability Standard for 5-kHz UHF DAMA Terminal Waveform, MIL-STD-188-182, September 1992.

Interoperability Standard for 25-kHz UHF DAMA Terminal Waveform, MIL-STD-188-183, September 1992.

Kleinrock, L., Queueing Systems, *Vol. I: Theory*, Wiley, 1975.

Kleinrock, L., Queueing Systems, *Vol. II: Computer Applications*, Wiley, 1976.

Konheim, Alan G., and Raymond Pickholtz, "Analysis of integrated voice/data multiplexing," *IEEE Transactions on Communications*, COM-32, pp. 140–147, February 1984.

Konheim, Alan G., and M. Reiser, "Analysis of a communication channel shared by synchronous connection and data unite processes," *Proceedings of the Conference on Teletraffic Analysis and Computer Performance Evaluation*, Amsterdam, pp. 375–394, 1986.

Kwong, R. H., and A. Leon-Garcia, "Performance analysis of an integrated hybrid-switched multiplex structure," *Performance Evaluation*, pp. 81–91, 1984.

Lee, H. W., and J. W. Mark, "Combined Random Reservation Access for Packet Switched Transmission Over a Satellite with On-Board Processing: Part I— Global Beam Satellite," *IEEE Transactions on Communications*, Vol. COM-31, No. 10, October 1983.

Li, V. O. K., and T. Y. Yan, "An integrated voice and data multiple-access scheme for a land-mobile satellite system," *Proceedings of the IEEE*, Vol. 72, No. 11, November 1984.

Maglaris B.S., and M. Schwartz, "Optimal fixed frame multiplexing in integrated line- and packet-switched communications networks," *IEEE Transactions on Information Theory*, IT-28, No. 2, pp. 262–272, March 1982.

McAuliffe, Amy, "Staying alive: rad-hard ICs continue to populate satellites," *Military and Aerospace Electronics*, March 1996.

Nelson, R., "Fast SRAMs keep pace with military applications," *Military and Aerospace Electronics*, November 1994.

Rabiner, L. R., "Applications of voice processing to telecommunications," *Proceedings of the IEEE*, Vol. 82, No. 2, February 1994.

Rafuse, R. P., *Rain-Outage Reduction by Data Storage in EHF SATCOM Systems*, MIT Lincoln Lab. Project Report DCA-10, November 25, 1980.

Raychaudhuri, D., and K. Joseph, "Performance evaluation of slotted Aloha with generalized retransmission backoff," *IEEE Trans. on Communications*, January 1990, Vol. 38, No. 1, pp. 117–122.

Sewell, Kelly, "SRAM makers strive to meet demands for faster, smaller devices," *Military and Aerospace Electronics*, October 1995.

"Solid-state gains ground," *Military and Aerospace Electronics*, February 1995.

Tanenbaum, A. S., *Computer Networks*, Prentice Hall, 1981.

Tijms, H.C., "Computational Methods for Queueing Models," *Queueing Theory and its Applications, Liber Amicorum for J. W. Cohen*, O. J. Boxma and R. Syski, eds., North-Holland, 1988.

Weinstein, C. J., M. L. Malpass, and M. J. Fisher, "Data traffic performance of an integrated circuit- and packet-switched multiplex structure," *IEEE Transactions on Communications*, COM-28, No. 6, pp. 873–878, 6 June 1980.

Weinstein, C. J., "Experience with speech communications in packet networks," *IEEE J. on Selected Areas in Communications*, Vol. SAC-1, No. 6, December 1983.

Wieselthier, J. E., and A. Ephremides, "A new class of protocols for multiple access in satellite networks," *IEEE Transactions on Automatic Control*, Vol. AC-25, No. 5, October 1980.

Wieselthier, J. E., and A. Ephremides, "Fixed- and movable-boundary channel-access schemes for integrated voice/data wireless networks," *IEEE Transactions on Communications*, Vol. 43, No. 1, January 1995.

Wolff, R. W., *Stochastic Modeling and the Theory of Queues*, Prentice Hall, 1989.

Wong, C. W., and S. Thanawastien, "Tree Conflict Resolution Algorithms on Multiple-Channel Networks," *Proceedings of the IEEE INFOCOM Conference*, 1987.

Xiong, F., "Modem techniques in satellite communications," *IEEE Communications Magazine*, August 1994.

Yao, D., "Refining the diffusion approximation for the M/G/m queue," *Operations Research*, Vol. 33, No. 6, pp. 1266–1277, 1985.

Ziemer, R. E., and R. L. Peterson, *Digital Communications and Spread Spectrum Systems*, Macmillan, 1985.

Zuk, William S., MIT Lincoln Laboratory Quarterly Review for MILSTAR Joint Program Office, September 1, 1995.